T0336330

PROPHETS OF LOVE

Advancing Studies in Religion

Series editor: Sarah Wilkins-Laflamme

Advancing Studies in Religion catalyzes and provokes original research in the study of religion with a critical edge. The series advances the study of religion in method and theory, textual interpretation, theological studies, and the understanding of lived religious experience. Rooted in the long and diverse traditions of the study of religion in Canada, the series demonstrates awareness of the complex genealogy of religion as a category and as a discipline. ASR welcomes submissions from authors researching religion in varied contexts and with diverse methodologies.

The series is sponsored by the Canadian Corporation for Studies in Religion whose constituent societies include the Canadian Society of Biblical Studies, Canadian Society for the Study of Religion, Canadian Society of Patristic Studies, Canadian Theological Society, Société canadienne de théologie, and Société québécoise pour l'étude de la religion.

PROPHETS OF LOVE

The Unlikely Kinship of

LEONARD COHEN

AND THE

Apostle Paul

Matthew R. Anderson

McGill-Queen's University Press

Montreal & Kingston | London | Chicago

ISBN 978-0-2280-1864-3 (cloth)
ISBN 978-0-2280-1865-0 (ePDF)
ISBN 978-0-2280-1866-7 (ePUB)

Legal deposit fourth quarter 2023
Bibliothèque nationale du Québec

Printed in Canada on acid-free paper that is 100% ancient forest free
(100% post-consumer recycled), processed chlorine free

This book has been published with the help of a grant from the Canadian
Federation for the Humanities and Social Sciences, through the Awards to
Scholarly Publications Program, using funds provided by the Social Sciences
and Humanities Research Council of Canada. Funding was also received from
Concordia University's Aid to Research-Related Events program, administered
by the Office of the Vice-President, Research and Graduate Studies.

We acknowledge the support of the Canada Council for the Arts.
Nous remercions le Conseil des arts du Canada de son soutien.

Library and Archives Canada Cataloguing in Publication

Title: Prophets of love : the unlikely kinship of Leonard Cohen and the
    Apostle Paul / Matthew Robert Anderson.
Names: Anderson, Matthew R. (Matthew Robert), author.
Series: Advancing studies in religion ; 15.
Description: Series statement: Advancing studies in religion ; 15
    Includes bibliographical references and index.
Identifiers: Canadiana (print) 20230206409 | Canadiana (ebook) 20230224393
    ISBN 9780228018643 (hardcover) | ISBN 9780228018650 (PDF)
    ISBN 9780228018667 (EPUB)
Subjects: LCSH: Cohen, Leonard, 1934–2016. | LCSH: Cohen, Leonard, 1934–
    2016—Religion. | LCSH: Paul, the Apostle, Saint. | LCSH: Paul, the Apostle,
    Saint—Jewish interpretations.
Classification: LCC PS8505.O22 Z52 2023 | DDC C811/.54—dc23

For Agata and Czarek

Contents

Acknowledgments

Leonard Cohen's final years were graced by public expressions of gratitude – and of penance – from which we all could learn. I am thankful to him for having produced so many beautiful words for me to analyze. The time during which I was waiting to hear if this work might be accepted for publication coincided with a summer course at Concordia University, Montreal. On those warm evenings, a down-town building painted with Cohen's face happened to be situated in such a way as to fill an entire window of my fifth-floor classroom. After teaching I'd look up and say: "Okay, Leonard. Whether this project goes ahead is up to you."

The conversation partner for Leonard whom you encounter in the book is Paul: equally problematic, and equally compelling, but for different reasons. I would never have distanced myself from the Paul of the church so as to get to know him as a first-century Jew had it not been for reading Krister Stendahl decades ago. I'm forever grateful to my then-professor, Irwin Buck, at the Lutheran Theological Seminary in Saskatoon, for introducing me to a perspective that would shape my academic life. Encounters on paper and meetings in person with other remarkable scholars since – Pamela Eisenbaum, Kathy Ehrensperger, Paula Fredriksen, and Mark Nanos, among others – have pushed forward and solidified that understanding.

Dr Sara Parks is my partner in all things. As a fellow fan of Leonard Cohen who is also a scholar of late Second Temple Judaism, *and* a talented writer, her careful reading of this manuscript and her suggestions and corrections have made it what it is. The book simply would not exist without her. Her friend, and mine, Zengetsu Myōkyō, from her own experiences of the Roshi, of Leonard Cohen, and of Mt Baldy, helped keep me from some errors that threatened the manuscript; I'm extremely thankful for her help.

I'm grateful to editor Kyla Madden at McGill-Queen's University Press for taking on this book, and to editorial assistant Lesley Trites as well as copy editor Susan Glickman for their corrections and commentary. Likewise, I wish to thank the two anonymous reviewers who greatly improved the work. Given the breadth of scholarship on both Leonard and Paul, there are bound to be omissions – they are my responsibility, and mine alone.

Beverly Smith-Wiltsie and the people of St Veronica's Parish, Dorval invited me years ago to give my first "Leonard and Paul" talk and seemed to enjoy it even though my reflections were only just beginning. A seed was planted then that has grown into this book. Thank you.

Thank you to the University Research Committee of Concordia University, Montreal for a grant which helped with the publication of this book, and to the Concordia University Part-Time Faculty Association (CUPFA) for a grant to help with indexing. I have been privileged over many years to have been so supported by Concordia in my research and writing.

This book is for all the scholars – most of them women, and many of them named above – who have so influenced and formed my view of Paul and of Leonard. I dedicate it especially to the scholar whose charming, cedar-kissed house Sara and I were so fortunate to stay in while I wrote this book: another fan of both Leonard and Paul, Dr Agata Bielik-Robson, professor of Jewish studies, University of Nottingham.

PROPHETS OF LOVE

1 Almost Like the Blues

Thoughts with My Feet up on Leonard Cohen's Coffee Table

Although Leonard Cohen and I shared the city of Montreal, I never met the poet, musician, and "bird on a wire." Through a twist of fate, my wife Sara wound up with several pieces of furniture from Cohen's former house on Rue Vallières. Leonard's Roshi had asked him to allow our friend, Zengetsu Myōkyō (another of the Mount Baldy monks), to establish the Montreal Zen Centre in Cohen's house. When the Centre later moved down the street, Leonard encouraged the abbess to stay on in his house. She remained until near Leonard's death, when she was asked to move out. Sara's station wagon was enlisted, and we ended up with the extra furniture. As I write this, I am sitting on a wicker chair from the place, my feet on a matching glass-topped coffee-table. One of my favourite photos of Leonard is of him in almost this position in 1974, barefooted, smiling, and reading a book by his friend Irving Layton.[1] We will keep this chair forever.

Not long ago, we had to downsize. We were forced to sell the little white brass bed that had made the same circuitous route from Cohen's home in Montreal's Plateau to our flat across the ocean. The British man who bought it told us his partner was a "massive fan" of Leonard Cohen. They planned to spray a clear lacquer over the peeling paint "so it will always stay just the way it is, right now." We explained that we had no idea whether Cohen had ever slept in the bed (although we knew that Kyōzan, the Zen Centre dog, frequently had). It didn't matter; the fact that the bed had been in Leonard's home was enough to render it sacred. Selling a used bed from a house owned by

Leonard Cohen counts as one of life's stranger experiences. Given his sense of humour, no doubt he would have appreciated the moment.[2]

I love Leonard Cohen. I am not alone. In the final years of his life, the poet and singer broke through to a remarkable level of public acclaim and warmth: what Myra Bloom calls a "full-blown canonization."[3] Long before his fedora-tipping final tour, and the release of *You Want It Darker* on his eighty-second birthday in 2016, Cohen had become as much icon as individual. Since his death shortly after, his reputation has only grown.

Perhaps like you, when I listen to Cohen's bleak and magnificent poetry, I find myself startled – sometimes to laughter, sometimes to regret, and most often to an appreciation of the dark, rich, sweetness of love and loss. There are lyrics on every one of his albums that move me. Many of the greatest treasures are his last works. In them his language is wistful, at times prayerful. Even biblical.[4] His unblinking observations of his inevitable end are made sweeter by how much pathos, humour, longing, and wisdom sit in almost every line of those final songs.

I admit there has always been something seductive in Leonard's love of longing, his longing in love, and the hints of his insider knowledge of both. I was a sucker for his act. With Leonard, you always knew that, on some level, you were being had, but you enjoyed it anyway. In his 1960s novel *The Favourite Game*, Leonard's main character and avatar Breavman states that he wants to relate to people like "a magician" and "a hypnotist," leaving his mark without himself being changed.[5] Like many others I was hypnotized by Leonard, listening in hopes of eventually understanding that "sweet unknowing" to which he gave voice. Through my own experiences of cancer and heartbreak, I had lived through enough to nod my head in agreement when he wrote "bitter liquor sweetens / In the hammered cup."[6]

There were always gaunt goodbyes in his work, and there was always charming forgiveness, but it felt as if these acts became less staged as Leonard aged. For him, growing old really was "one of the most compassionate ways of saying goodbye."[7] I deeply empathized, and still do, with his lines:

> and here is a voice
> I have been listening to
> for a long time
> it says: O G-d, I love you
> it says: Child, I love you back.[8]

And yet.

Despite my admiration, I know that I might not always have *liked* everything about Leonard Cohen in person. This is especially true of the younger man. When one is attentive to issues of gender and power, there are many, many lines in Leonard's writings and much in his biography that causes discomfort. He himself referred to his failings. Yet somehow he managed to transform those faults into lyrics rather than litigation, perhaps by presenting himself with apparent vulnerability and carefully-framed remorse.[9] *Rolling Stone* reporter Mikal Gilmore writes: "He always aspired to better angels, but he also admitted to – in fact, took a certain relief and pride in – an honest assessment of his less merciful side. On the late albums, he was not simply proclaiming prayers but also saw a duty for penance."[10] Johanna Schneller is less generous in her article about Cohen and the #MeToo movement.[11] However, she allows that the elderly Leonard "finally grew into the empath he pretended to be."[12] Myra Bloom argues for a "more complex understanding of a man who, before he became divine, was obsessed with the flesh, and not always in ways that are palatable today."[13]

This book began when I realized there was something oddly familiar about my discomfort with, yet admiration for, Leonard Cohen. There was an uncomfortable tension between being inspired by his mastery of language and his artistic opus, while feeling aware of and scandalized by his flaws. It hit me where I had felt this before: it's how

I feel about the Apostle Paul.[14] Noticing Leonard's shortcomings became the first step in exploring what turned out to be some surprising similarities between the cohen[15] and the apostle. You may note that throughout what follows, I will generally use the name "Leonard" instead of "Cohen" or "Leonard Cohen." I do this to balance it better with "Paul."

My PhD is in Pauline studies. I love Paul too. Year after year, I try to bring his words alive for my students. But after decades of studying, teaching, and researching his life and letters, I know I would almost certainly not get along with Paul in person. Paul was volatile. He could be rather bad-mannered. Leonard apparently made an excellent dinner partner – Paul likely did not. Leonard was courtly, Paul's writings suggest he was much less so. At least in his later years Leonard possessed unfailing old-school charm, while Paul seems abrasive to us, even in his more irenic letters. Paul's consistently polemical correspondence tells us he was often in conflict. Take, for instance, his letter to the Galatians. If it were an email, it would have been written in "all caps." As for being inappropriate, in that letter he actually suggests his opponents castrate themselves![16]

All our surviving evidence concerning Paul shows him to have been as argumentative as Leonard was diplomatic. To contemporary ears, Paul's writing is frequently caustic and belittling and his comments imperious or, alternatively, passive-aggressive. Paul wrote that he preferred to preach where no one else had already established an assembly.[17] He makes it sound as if it is for the good of his message, but one suspects he had a problem getting along with others.[18] Yet it was this same prickly character who wrote the sublime hymn that is 1 Corinthians chapter thirteen, ending with "now faith, hope, and love abide, these three; and the greatest of these is love."[19]

Leonard and Paul: both are revered, one as a saint and the other as an artist. One is a first-century figure, one a twenty-first. Cohen was a physically small man and Paul reportedly so as well; recent research through the lens of disability suggests Paul may have been of *very* short stature.[20] But both were bigger than life in every other way. One is a self-described "slave of Jesus Christ" and "apostle," apostle being a title you may be surprised to know that other apostles did not want to give Paul.[21] The other disarmingly wrote about himself (even while he worked through physical pain to produce his music and poetry right up to his death), that he was a "sportsman and a shepherd, [a] lazy bastard living in a suit."[22]

At first, linking the two might seem a stretch.[23] However, once one starts, the parallels between Leonard and Paul are so many, and the differences (of course there *are* differences!) so telling, that putting them side by side quickly moves from the entertaining to the illuminating. The similarities are particularly weighty when we think of their common Judaism. Both were born, *and remained,* Jewish. This is one of the main points I wish to make in this book. Yet Leonard's lyrics continue to quite often be interpreted through a Christian lens. And as for Paul: as John G. Gager puts it, nothing "has produced more animosity between Jews and Christians" than history's usual and mistaken Christianized readings of Paul.[24]

Years ago, I gave a series of talks titled "He's Our Man: Why Leonard Cohen and St Paul Were Secretly Brothers." I tried to make the case that comparing Paul and an increasingly venerated Leonard tells us much about both. I believe that has become even more true since Cohen's death. History has yet to make its final judgements. But living in Montreal, where statues of Paul and forty-foot-high murals of Leonard both look down in blessing on passers-by, might have helped make this book's connection.

First things first: with Leonard as with Paul, the writings are not the person.[25] At least, not exactly.[26] Leonard called himself "lazy." Paul described himself as "unimpressive." Both statements are demonstrably false. Paul attracted the groups that became the seeds of Western Christianity, and writings by, about, or attributed to him form more than half of the collection known as the New Testament. Leonard's daily regime and his artistic output show that he was the opposite of lazy.[27] We have to be careful in thinking Paul deeply felt every sentiment he expressed, or that Leonard's every lyric is autobiographical. Whether for the purpose of persuasion or poetry, a writer has license.

What follows then, is not a biography of each man. Instead, I have tried to stick to analyzing their *written* work. It is important to note that over the years, the thinking of both developed. This can be seen as much in Paul's writings as in Leonard's, although Leonard's documented career spanned many more years. In his final poetry, he comes to peace with the meaning of his life and work in the face of a death he can feel approaching. It reminds me of what was likely Paul's final known letter, to the Jesus followers in Rome. There he too seems to be taking a deep breath and, especially in light of what may have been some spectacular failures for him, summing up his life's work.

Both Paul and Leonard were Jews, and both were religious. Among the wide varieties of human religious practice, both men lived and wrote from the mystical end of the spectrum. Both made their faith a discipline and a practice. Both were simultaneously insiders and outsiders to their Jewish communities. Both made their way, and their reputations, in the wider, non-Jewish, world, and both became famous in that world (Paul after his death, Leonard before). Both men were complicated – if very different – in their masculinities, and both were ambiguous in how they saw and treated women. Both had a special interest in Jesus and were obsessed with the God of Israel. Both struggled in different ways with the image and meaning of the cross. While both have been accused otherwise, each remained Jewish in their worship, their words, their obsessions, and their anticipations, to their dying day.

From childhood, both Paul and Leonard ate, drank, and breathed the language of the Hebrew scriptures. "I was born in the heart of the bible / and I know the holy pitch," writes Leonard.[28] Perhaps this refers to his Jewish name "Eliezer," which occurs in several places in the Torah, the core of the Jewish Bible. The images and rhythms of ancient, biblical speech echo through the writings of Leonard and Paul. They repurpose figures from the Hebrew Bible such as David and Abraham to make their own points. And both drift into the language of Jewish prayer, from Hallelujah to Hineni.[29]

Occasionally, my undergraduate students write essays in which, as soon as they mention God, they begin to use archaic terms like "thee" and "thou" – language they certainly do not use with their friends! For the students it is semantic drift, an unconscious mistake. But in the hands of a poet like Leonard, or a writer like Paul, such language is hardly accidental. Their carefully deployed biblical phrasing taps into reservoirs of deep symbolic meaning.[30] When Leonard talks about "the waters" parting and writes "I was taken out of Egypt,"[31] or Paul mentions "first fruits,"[32] they knew the complex set of accompanying connotations such allusions to Pesach and to Shavu'ot would spark in the minds of their hearers.

Neither was averse to taking the point of view of the divine. They even claimed to speak *for* the divine – what is called "prophetic speech."[33] Moral philosopher and theologian Timothy P. Jackson declares Leonard Cohen "the closest thing … to a biblical prophet."[34] Paul wrote to followers who were threatening to abandon his teachings: "I want you to know, brothers and sisters, that the gospel that was proclaimed by me is not of human origin."[35] Leonard once playfully challenged fellow poet Peter Dale Scott about divine voice in "You Want It Darker": "Who says 'i' want it darker?" he wrote. "Who says the 'you' is me?"[36]

For both Leonard and Paul, the written word was the primary medium through which prophetic truths were delivered. In sentences that rubbed shoulders they expressed everything from the humorous to the ironic to the petty, all in service to revelations of the sublime. Each powerfully portrayed love, sacrifice, suffering, brokenness, and, ultimately, redemption. Facing the darkness while yearning for and pointing toward a divine if somewhat ambiguous light occurs constantly in both their writings. In thrall to what they believed to be a divine message, they polished their art while connecting the divine to the human condition.

While no one would deny that each writer possessed natural talent, some may not be aware that each also put significant labour into the science and art of persuasive speech. Leonard may have had a reputation as an uninspired student, but he did become president of the McGill University debating union.[37] And despite Paul's self-deprecation concerning his speaking abilities (calculated self-deprecation being another trait the two share), his letters are full of trademark first-century rhetorical devices that may demonstrate a relatively privileged level of education.[38]

Above all, the similarity that launched this book was how diligently each worked to encourage warm identification with their audiences, despite suffering very public moments of relational failure and raw vulnerability.[39] Both sometimes mystified their co-workers, caused hurt, were betrayed by insiders, and publicly split from friends and allies. Yet the simple fact of Paul's Christ-assemblies[40] and Leonard's audiences tell us that each also had a powerful magnetism. Friends of Leonard almost universally describe him as having been thoughtful, courtly, and generous.[41] Both could also reportedly sometimes be off-putting in person. Several of my women acquaintances were markedly unimpressed after encounters with the mid-life Cohen. Paul admits that some found him "contemptible."[42]

The fact is that famous figures can hardly be separated from their public personas. As time passes, the more irretrievable the historical persons become. This might even be the way they wanted it.[43] Especially near the end of his life, Leonard let his lyrics stand for him as apologies and eulogies, perhaps as a way of negotiating how history might otherwise judge his relations, especially to the women in his life. And as New Testament scholar Joseph Marchal cheekily quips: "Paul is probably the least interesting thing about Paul's letters."[44] For reasons about which we can only speculate, Paul seemed to prefer to let his letters do the talking. Despite this, it was his increasingly mythologized life that became paradigmatic for so many later Christians.[45]

To this point I've been cataloguing similarities between Leonard and Paul – however, if we turn to their relationships to women, you may think the difference is enough to scuttle the comparison! Paul's view of sex ranges from tolerant to negative. His reputation as a women-hater, however, is historically inaccurate, as we will see in chapter 4. Leonard's reputation is the opposite, to the point of legend. Leonard's wry combination of salvation and sex ("I knelt there at the delta")[46] was hardly Paul's ascetic message: "I wish that all were [celibate] as I myself am."[47] Mikal Gilmore's 2016 *Rolling Stone* retrospective posits that Leonard's life's work, and his tempestuous love affairs, were all directed by "an ideal of romantic meaning and passion."[48] Christophe Lebold makes the argument that Leonard was marketed as the self-designated "troubadour" of existentialist love.[49] By contrast, Paul seemed to have been untouched by romance. He called even married people to follow him in his sexual asceticism.[50] His only burning passion was for the one he called Christ his Lord, and for the God of Israel.

Paul's ambivalent views of sex echo ascetic strands of early Judaism, but his supposedly negative views of women do not. Paul has not only been accused of being a misogynist, but very nearly of being the person primarily responsible for the long history of the mistreatment of women in the later Christian church. This reputation has falsely tarnished the apostle, as we will see in chapter 4. On the other hand, while Leonard's lyrics more than occasionally participate in gender stereotypes, and his novels are increasingly unacceptable to contemporary readers,[51] no one ever accused him of ignoring women. On the contrary, he was fanatically observant of, and obsessed with women, from his teenaged writing to his dying days.[52]

In this book, I invite you to imagine Leonard and Paul – in their differences and their similarities – as siblings, separated at birth by centuries and cultures. Through the words of Cohen (whose family name means "priest") and Paul, who once wrote he was engaged in a "priestly service,"[53] I would like to introduce you, or re-introduce you, perhaps, to these two poets of divine and human love.[54] In each of the chapters that follow, I highlight one thematic point of comparison in what their writings reveal. Taken together, these chapters build an introduction to some of the latest scholarship on Paul. They also shed new light on the profound depths of religious thinking underlying and inspiring Leonard's lyrics.

To help in your own drawing of connections, I've paired texts from each author as "primary source meditations" at the end of each chapter. A Leonard meditation may seem odd. However, this is how millions of people around the world continue to receive and revere Cohen's works.[55] Those fortunate enough to attend one of his final concerts would likely understand why "more than one reviewer had likened Leonard's concerts, the quiet, the jubilation, the sense of grace, the reverence for the beauty of the word, to religious gatherings."[56] My wife, also a professor of religious studies, but who has worked in multi-faith chaplaincy, said that his final concert in Montreal was "unquestionably a sacred space."

For those familiar with the New Testament, a Paul meditation may seem more commonplace. However, my hope is that setting his words beside Leonard's will dislodge both from stereotype and assumption. Seeing "old ideas" in new ways was what both characters were after.

There are so many beautiful lines from both Leonard and Paul that comparing, contrasting, and analyzing their writing at times feels like diluting it. As A.M. Klein, another Montreal poet who appeared with Cohen on an early CBC Spoken Word album,[57] once wrote: "One soon realizes that quotation would prolong analysis interminably."[58] But what joy in letting them speak! Fans of Leonard and/or Paul's works will no doubt have opinions on the texts I have chosen to analyze – and the many I have omitted. That is part of what makes these two so interesting. I encourage you to think of other Pauline passages, or Leonard lines, that corroborate or contest some of the comparisons I've made.

In the end, I hope you will agree that spending time with one poet of love, brokenness, and hope, can help us encounter the other. Leonard's twenty-first century description of his calling could as easily apply to Paul, whose first-century visions changed both him and the world:

I've had the invitation
that a sinner can't refuse
It's almost like salvation
It's almost like the blues.[59]

TEXT MEDITATION

Listen to: "Almost Like the Blues," *Popular Problems* (2014).

On the topic of the intentional and practised artistry one can find in both Leonard and Paul, compare:

I was always working steady
But I never called it art
I was funding my depression
Meeting Jesus reading Marx
Sure it failed my little fire
But it's bright the dying spark
Go tell the young messiah
What happens to the heart
    ("Happens to the Heart," *The Flame*, 3)

You remember our labour and toil, brothers and sisters
We worked night and day, so that we might not burden any
    of you
While we proclaimed to you the good news of God.
    (1 Thessalonians 2:9)

FURTHER READING

A good biography of Cohen is Simmons's *I'm Your Man: The Life of Leonard Cohen*, published by Vintage/Penguin/Random House first in 2012, with new material added in 2017 after Cohen's death. Simon & Schuster has a three-volume series devoted to a life of Cohen, all written by Michael Posner, called *Leonard Cohen, Untold Stories*. An enjoyable and accessible graphic novel presentation of Cohen's life and career is Girard's *Leonard Cohen: On a Wire*, also and originally in French.

Harry Freedman's *Leonard Cohen: The Mystical Roots of Genius* is a masterful exploration of many of the same themes I'm presenting here. As I've tried to do, Freedman avoids dissecting Cohen's motivations by reflecting instead on his sources, particularly the treasures of the Bible and of religious tradition. This is a must-read for anyone interested in Leonard Cohen's spirituality.

As you might expect about a person two millennia removed from us, an accurate life of Paul is harder to come by. In addition to the time gap, the problem is that while Paul certainly was not shy to write about himself, he didn't dwell on biographical details. When Paul did write about his intentions, travels, Jewish theology, or mystical visions, it was always to build towards some other persuasive point. To further muddy the waters, there are several New Testament letters that claim to be (or were assumed to be) by Paul but were pseudonymously written much later. Additional ancient writings about Paul, and hints as to the historical person in works such as *The Acts of Paul and Thecla*, also postdate Paul by decades or, in some cases, centuries. Most scholars now believe that even the New Testament book of Acts cannot reliably be used as a source of biographical information about Paul; it was likely written a half-century after his death. Moreover, ancient historians did not write with the same interests – including the concern for accuracy – as today. Simmons interviewed over a hundred people close to Leonard Cohen while researching her book

– childhood friends, lovers, and fellow singers and poets. While the author of Luke and Acts notes his concern to give what he calls "an orderly account" and to use eyewitnesses, writing history was not the same then as now. Many ancient historians, such as Thucydides, considered it best practice to invent speeches and put them into the mouths of the main characters (he says as much in his *Peloponnesian War* 1.22, for instance). What was important was whether the author crafted a work that caught the historical *significance* of the character.

That said, non-specialist readers interested in learning more about Paul would do well to visit the Society of Biblical Literature's "Bible Odyssey" web resource. Davina Lopez writes an excellent introduction to Paul there: https://www.bibleodyssey.org/people/main-articles/paul. Finally, my own article, "Paul and Pauline Epistles" can be found in *The Encyclopedia of Ancient History*.

It perhaps should go without saying but if you are interested in Leonard's writing, I encourage you to start with the works themselves, either the books which I quote throughout this study, or the albums which contain so much of his poetry.

2 Let Us Compare Mythologies

Leonard and Paul within Judaism

After Leonard died in November 2016, he was quietly mourned in a synagogue ceremony. Before most of us had even heard of the death, the star whom millions admired was privately buried in a family plot. Those who expected a public, secular service should not have been surprised. The Hebrew name "Cohen" denotes a Jewish priestly lineage, a fact of which Leonard was well aware, even at a young age.[1] "I had a very Messianic childhood," he once said, "I was told I was a descendant of Aaron, the High Priest."[2] Some of Leonard's first poems were typed out at a desk side by side with his maternal grandfather, Rabbi Solomon Klaniski-Kline, a noted religious scholar.[3] He and Leonard would sometimes go through the book of Isaiah together and compare notes (Cohen has a piece called "Isaiah" in his volume *Stranger Music*, although in fact it refers to the Song of Songs as much as the prophet). Important for the family was also the fact that Leonard's paternal great-grandfather Lazarus Cohen helped found Montreal's Congregation Shaar Hashomayim.

In other words, Leonard was not only Jewish, but he had *yichus* (pedigree) and deep roots in the Montreal Jewish community. Rich knowledge of ancestral themes and literature permeates his work. His first lines in *Let Us Compare Mythologies* – a title which, notably, anticipates this book – refer to both the Shoah (Holocaust) and the Torah. His final album *You Want It Darker* features the cantor and choir of Shaar Hashomayim backing him while he sings *Hineni*. *Hineni* ("Here I am") is traditionally a prayer of preparation chanted on Rosh Hashanah. It occurs in key moments in Genesis, Exodus, Samuel, and Isaiah.

From first to last, Leonard's work was Jewish. Despite how the Catholicism of his childhood nannies, the Buddhism of his Zen practice on Mount Baldy, and religious themes taken from Sufism also feature in his poetic imagery, his Judaism was never in doubt – at least, not for him.[4] Montreal is ripe for such blends. Leonard's career tapped into what Stacey Engels describes as "the city's inherent juxtapositions: old synagogues on streets named for saints, steeples towering over sex clubs, stone angels spray-painted with the circle-A of anarchy."[5] Behind it all, Leonard saw the divine.

Publicly, however, Leonard was as coy about his religion as his love of specific women. He once teased reporters: "I am very close to myself so I can say with great authority that I am not religious."[6] In private, his remarks reveal perhaps truer feelings: he mentioned to his rabbi, Mordecai Finley, "that he thought everything he wrote was liturgy."[7] Leonard's time as a Buddhist monk, alongside his consistent use of Christian images, might have led some to think of him as a religious tourist,[8] but anyone who drank so deeply of the sources could be nothing of the sort. His poem "Not a Jew" begins with the words "Anyone who says I'm not a Jew is not a Jew."[9] It was particularly during and after *Book of Mercy* (1984), that he emphasized his deep belonging within Judaism.

By contrast, Paul stated his religious affiliations so loudly and clearly that it's a bit surprising that history consistently got it so wrong. He notes with pride that he was a Jew who was "circumcised on the eighth day, a member of the people of Israel, of the tribe of Benjamin, a Hebrew born of Hebrews."[10] The God Paul is claiming is the same God of Israel he believed had spoken to the patriarchs and the prophets. Even while writing to non-Jews, when Paul wants to prove a point, he quotes Jewish texts and uses Jewish examples almost exclusively. He saw himself squarely within Jewish tradition.

The fact that, like Leonard, Paul also lived and died a Jew has been consistently overlooked for nearly two millennia by the many who wanted to declare him, too, to have been a Christian. Ironically, Paul "as the first Christian" is an image that served both Christianity and Judaism in the early centuries in which they sought to distinguish themselves from each other. It's one of the tragedies of history that so few realize that Paul was born, lived, and died, not rejecting first-century Judaism but working within one strand of it.[11] That Paul is best known to us for his teachings about Jesus – another Torah-observant Jew – shouldn't hide that fact.

Down through the centuries, Paul's admirers claimed him as the first Christian, while his critics derided him for the same thing.[12] But the undoubtedly radical change of life Paul went through after his vision of the risen Christ was never a conversion *away* from Judaism to a different faith.[13] For one thing, Christianity didn't yet exist. At the time, the Jesus movement was simply one school of Torah interpretation among many within Judaism, one apocalyptic timeline among several, one hoped-for Jewish redeemer among a variety of contenders.[14] Just as importantly, the themes Paul preached, themes such as resurrection, atonement, repentance, the judgment of the nations, and the coming of a messiah were all Jewish themes.[15] They *became* Christian themes over the four centuries that followed. In Paul's lifetime, there was nothing un-Jewish about them.

The idea that Paul converted to a new religion and taught that Jews were replaced by Christians as the people of God has long been at the core of historic Christianity. Such a view is called "supersessionism." Supersessionism relies on stereotype and mistakes some basic facts of history; it leads to white supremacy and violence. Historically, it paved the way for Christian genocide against Jews.[16]

In later chapters we will unfold how Paul's "conversion" is a misinterpretation. For now, it's important to remember how Paul's message of Jesus and his urgency about the last days originally had a natural home within one of the branches of the diverse Judaism of his day. Like Leonard, Paul saw himself in relation to and under the call of the God who had first called Abraham and Sarah, and who gave the Torah to a specific community through Moses. The fact that Paul's assemblies were made up primarily of non-Jews shouldn't hide those deeply Jewish roots. Jewish communities had been accustomed to attracting non-Jewish admirers and "god-fearing" adherents for centuries.[17]

———

Both Leonard and Paul were interested in attracting non-Jews. For Paul, it was specifically to convince them to renounce their gods and join the Jesus movement as a way of worshipping the God of Israel. Leonard had no such apocalyptic urgency. For him, the interest was in attracting audiences (and occasionally, lovers).

Paul felt *called* to communicate to non-Jews. This is the one constant we can identify in all his letters. He wrote that he was destined to speak to the nations (the word "nations" is synonymous with "gentiles" in New Testament Greek):

> But when God, who had set me apart before I was born
> and called me through his grace,
> was pleased to reveal his Son to me,
> so that I might proclaim him to the Gentiles …[18]

Paul felt himself to be in a long line of Jewish prophets, but with the wrinkle that he had been sent in the final days to prophesy *outward* to the nations, instead of inward to fellow Jews. Like Jonah, who was sent to Assyrians rather than Israelites, such prophets were not necessarily happy to be called,[19] but ultimately had to submit to the irresistible demand of the God of Abraham, Ruth, and Moses. The heart of Judaism is the Torah, and the written work of Leonard and Paul shows that each in their own way felt a compulsion to express Torah in ways non-Jewish audiences could understand.[20] Leonard wrote this in an email to his friends in 2016, within months of his death:

he will make it darker
he will make it light
according to his torah
which leonard did not write[21]

Leonard signed the email with the Jewish name he'd been given at birth – Eliezer – meaning, "God is help."[22] The Montreal lad who had formed a country and western band called "The Buckskin Boys" with his gentile friends shared a name with one of the Maccabees. The Maccabees were the Jewish family which in 167 BCE led the overthrow of the Syrian-Greek monarch Antiochus IV. Eleazer and his family's successful resistance against Antiochus's attempts to outlaw Jewish worship and practice, and the Maccabees' cleansing and re-dedication of the Temple in Jerusalem, is commemorated every year at Hannukah. It's notable that a cosmopolitan figure like Leonard, who moved so easily through the non-Jewish world, held on to the fact that his Jewish name echoed a figure who strenuously resisted cultural and religious assimilation.[23]

Like Leonard, Paul was also a city person. Paul lived and breathed the ancient urban environment of the *polis* (city). Both men were raised thinking and expressing themselves not in Hebrew but in the international languages of their day: English for Leonard, and common (or "koine") Greek for Paul.[24] For both urbanites in particularly pluralistic times, the whole of the known world was backdrop and arena. Each in his own way was cosmopolitan.[25] Young Leonard moved to New York as soon as he was able to leave Montreal, then booked a flight for London when he received a Canada Council grant for emerging writers. The yearning that a very young Leonard penned in his first book of poetry soon came true: "O cities of the Decapolis across the Jordan / you are too great; our young men love you."[26]

For the rest of his life he was on the move, whether it was writing poetry on his beloved island in Greece, on world tours promoting albums, on international flights from Montreal or Los Angeles to visit his children in France, sitting zazen at Mount Baldy, or studying in India. Although Paul did not travel first-class, as Leonard often did, his letters show him constantly moving. His best-known correspondence is written from and to cities around the Aegean, not so far from Leonard's Hydra. Paul too followed the major travel arteries of his day, among others the Roman-built *Via Egnatia*.[27] Just as Leonard settled briefly here and there, Paul's time on the road was interspersed by stints in the major cities of the eastern Mediterranean.

Both men show the richness of the kinds of nested identities we all inherit. Paul was Jewish, Greek-cultured, and a Roman subject, all at once. This shouldn't be any more surprising than that Leonard was Jewish, an Anglo-Québecois, and North American. Many ancient Jews lived and dreamt in Greek back then, just as many Jews live and dream in English (and other non-Hebrew languages) today. On top of Leonard's bedrock Judaism – among other things he tried to keep kosher and took care to celebrate Shabbat meals with his children – he, like Paul, was happy to expose himself to a wide range of influences.[28] On his death, his friend Leon Wieseltier wrote in the *New York Times*: "We sometimes read and studied together, Lorca and midrash and Eluard and Buddhist scriptures and Cavafy. We could get quite Talmudic, especially with wine."[29]

Then how to explain the important, nuanced, and ongoing ways that Zen Buddhism influenced Leonard? The short answer is: Zen is not a religion, but a practice. It might be thought of in some ways as similar to ancient philosophies, which one could practice relatively independently of one's cultic obligations. In other words, Leonard was Jewish, *and also* Zen Buddhist.[30] Similarly, Paul was Jewish, *and also* influenced, for example, by then-popular forms of Stoicism.[31] Both individuals were able to dress traditional religious identity in new garments of language and culture. Both were very aware that this was what they were doing. Paul says he is willing to be "all things to all people."[32] Compare this to a lesser-known verse from Leonard's "Hallelujah": "It doesn't matter which you heard, the holy, or the broken, Hallelujah!"[33]

Both Paul and Leonard play with the ancient idea of how their God's "naming" gives strength and identity. Both intimately knew the words of Isaiah 43:1: "I have called you by name, you are mine." For both, a divine naming is the sign of, if not redemption, at least of its promise. Fans of Leonard's work can point out an even more notable use of the Name in Cohen's lyrics in the work "Love Itself." There, influenced not only by the Judaism he shared with Paul (and the Torah's creation story of creation from the earth), but also by the Buddhism of his Zen master, Kyozan Joshu Sasaki Roshi, Leonard wrote:

> In streams of light I clearly saw
> The dust you seldom see,
> Out of which the Nameless makes
> A name for one like me.[34]

Judaism and Christianity are different religions. *Now.* They weren't in Paul's lifetime.[35] Most of the New Testament was written by Jews who happened to be followers of Jesus. This is where some observers of Cohen still go wrong. For instance, in an article published shortly after his death, Sean Curnyn wrote: "Cohen is an Old Testament poet who can comprehend the New Testament without great strain or contradiction."[36] Curnyn is emphasizing an overly simple dichotomy. The reason Leonard could do this is that *much of the New Testament consists of Jewish documents*.[37] Non-Jews were only a small minority in the first few decades of the Jesus movements which gave rise to the New Testament and to the Christian Church.

Paul focussed his efforts on small groups of gentiles, not on his fellow Jews.[38] For the non-Jews to whom he preached, Paul's message was simple: they must give up their own gods.[39] This was a risky thing to do in the ancient world, since spurned local gods tended to be vengeful and to bring misfortune on cities and regions. Non-Jewish Christ followers could be, and were, blamed by their neighbours for natural disasters.[40] Paul required that these non-Jews turn to the God of Israel, the "living and true God" and "wait for his son from heaven, whom he raised from the dead, Jesus, who rescues us from the wrath that is coming."[41]

Following long traditions of varied Jewish reflection on how Judaism and the nations were related, other apostles questioned both Paul and the terms under which a non-Jew could follow Jesus.[42] Surely, some wondered, to follow a Jewish rabbi and deliverer, one would have to convert to a fully Torah-abiding lifestyle (if it were even possible for a non-Jew to convert to Judaism)?[43] After all, Jesus was a Jewish messiah sent by the Jewish God to the Jewish people in what his followers felt was a fulfillment of Jewish Scriptures. Jesus himself had followed Jewish customs, gathered Jewish disciples, interpreted the Torah, and been one of many reformers of the Jewish Temple. The movement Jesus founded seemingly *only* included Jewish people. Those non-Jews who wanted to follow Jesus would have to become Jews (proselytes) first.[44] This appeared obvious to some in the earliest movement – for instance, it seems to be the position taken by the competing Christ-preachers Paul refers to so sarcastically in Galatians.[45] However, laying such obligations on Christ-following non-Jews was not apparent to Paul.

Despite the long history of later Christian assumptions to the contrary, Paul firmly held that he and his fellow Jews should continue to follow Torah.[46] However, Paul's obsession concerning the place of non-Jews in God's plan, and misunderstandings concerning Paul's contradictory-sounding statements arising from his concern to include non-Jews without the necessity of their circumcision,[47] led to problems between him and other Jesus-missionaries. Against others in the movement that he himself admitted that he joined "late," Paul passionately believed non-Jews should be included in every way in the covenant, *as non-Jews who had kept their identity yet turned to the God of Israel.* For most of Christian history, interpreters have mistakenly assumed the opposite – that Paul was trying to convert *everyone* to a Torah-free practice.[48] The result was that Christians have long denigrated Torah observance and falsely contrasted it with God's grace, a casual and often unconscious anti-Judaism that characterizes Jews as pedantic rule-followers and prepares the ground for more vicious forms of anti-Semitism and oppression.

Like Leonard's, Paul's Jewishness has always been hidden in plain sight.[49] Yet almost "all later readers – Christian, Jewish, and other – have assumed that Paul stands behind the anti-Judaism of later New Testament writings and of mainstream Christianity."[50] Nietzsche, for instance, criticized Paul as the "apostle of hate." The fact that most contemporary Christians still understand Paul to have instigated the idea that Christians "replaced" Jews as God's special people, and the horrific anti-Semitic consequences of that theory of succession,[51] shows us just how important and dangerous our presuppositions can be.

Paul the Jew was obsessed with Christ. So was Leonard. Paul was a Christ-follower. Leonard was not. If Leonard was born, lived, and died Jewish, knowing the damage Christian beliefs have caused Jews, then why *his* fascination with Jesus? We will explore this in the next chapter. Certainly, Leonard's lyrics show that he was acutely aware of the overlap between Judaism and Christianity, and the rich heritage of shared scriptures. Jackson states: "For centuries, Christian theologians have appropriated Hebrew texts, awkwardly, as pointing forward to Jesus as the Messiah. At last, with Cohen, we have a Jewish thinker who quotes Christian texts, deftly, as harkening backward to their Hebraic origins. This is enormously courageous and profoundly therapeutic. He helps lead the Biblical tradition toward wholeness."[52]

For now, it's important to note that Leonard's attraction to Jesus did not mean he was attracted to Christianity as a faith. Cohen once said about his poetry: "You know the story of that juggler who performed his acrobatics and plate balancing in front of a statue of the virgin? Well, I think it really comes down to that. You really do what sings."[53] From Jesus to Joan of Arc, it was Christianity's rich store of images that Leonard loved.

TEXT MEDITATION

Listen to: "Born in Chains," *Popular Problems* (2014).

Compare:

> Blessed is the Name
> The Name be blessed
> Written on my heart
> In burning Letters
> That's all I know
> I cannot read the rest.[54]
>> ("Born in Chains," *The Flame,* 138–9)

> But whatever anyone dares to boast of – I am speaking as
>> a fool –
> I also dare to boast of that.
> Are they Hebrews? So am I.
> Are they Israelites? So am I.
> Are they descendants of Abraham? So am I.
> Are they ministers of Messiah (Christ)? I am talking like a
>> madman – I
> Am a better one …
>> (2 Corinthians 11:21b–23a)

> Think of us this way, as servants of Christ and stewards of the
>> divine mysteries of God.
>> (1 Corinthians 4:1)

FURTHER READING

One of the most helpful developments in the field known as Pauline studies is how, starting around the 1990s, more and more Jewish scholars began to look closely at Paul. They are part of a movement to read Paul within his own context, in the first century, and in a period known as the "late Second Temple period" of Judaism. See, for example, Fredriksen's "Paul and Judaism."

This book generally follows this "Paul within Judaism" approach to the ancient figure. While not all scholars in this group agree on everything (Isn't that always the case?), the general outlines are clear: a) Paul's own letters show that he was born, lived, worked, and died within Judaism; b) Paul's life-changing vision of the risen messiah (Jesus) did not take him outside of Judaism. Rather, Paul's encounter with Christ caused him to believe that the ancient Jewish notion of the history-ending Day of the Lord and its attendant resurrection of the dead was at hand and that he had a prophetic-style calling to announce this to the "nations," or non-Jewish world; and c) Paul's anti-Torah statements were intended only for his non-Jewish audience and not against Torah observance for Jews.

If you'd like to read more about the "Paul within Judaism" view, start by having a look at the helpful website https://marknanos.com/. You might also listen to Fredriksen's very short introduction to the subject of Paul within Judaism here: https://vimeo.com/144241054. For additional scholarly reading from the "Paul within Judaism" perspective, see also Eisenbaum, *Paul Was Not a Christian*, Gager, *Reinventing Paul*, and the classic early study, Stendahl, *Paul among Jews and Gentiles*.

An extremely helpful resource for teachers and students of the New Testament can be found in Vanden Eykel, Rollens, and Warren, eds, *Judeophobia and the New Testament*.

3 Lonely Wooden Tower

Leonard and Paul's Preoccupation with Jesus

Leonard and Paul share an obsession with Jesus. Paul identified so strongly with him that he once wrote, "It is no longer I who live but Christ who lives in me."[1] Leonard called Jesus "the most beautiful guy who ever walked the face of this earth."[2] While a deep investment in Jesus is exactly what you would imagine from the man some call the founder of Christianity, who is also the author of much of what later became the New Testament, such an attachment is not what one would automatically expect from a Montreal Jewish poet who knew the good, but also the bad, that has come from Christianity as a religion.

Paul represents a part of the early movement which focussed more on the messianic "Christ" than on the person Jesus had been, or what Jesus had done. Leonard, by contrast, was interested in the *man* Jesus of Nazareth, both as a sympathetic admirer and an artist interested in metaphor. Their obsessions met and overlapped at the focal point of the cross. The cross is central to the writings of both figures, even if the lessons they take from Jesus and his death look quite different.

In 1955, a young Leonard won a McGill University poetry competition with "For Wilf and His House." He opens with the words:

When young the Christians told me
how we pinned Jesus
like a lovely butterfly against the wood,
and I wept beside paintings of Calvary
at velvet wounds
and delicate twisted feet.[3]

Leonard came by the images in "For Wilf and His House" naturally. As a child, he was sometimes taken to church by his Christian nanny. Simmons quotes Leonard saying: "I love Jesus ... Always did, even as a kid."[4] The family's maid was an Irish Catholic; anyone who has spent any time in Montreal knows how rich the city is with Catholic tradition.[5]

The lines of his early poetry foreshadow two elements that would recur throughout Leonard's writing on Jesus: a highly positive but non-divine view of Jesus (a lovely butterfly, delicate twisted feet), and Leonard's self-identification as an outsider ("*we* pinned Jesus"). The poem did well. It was one of those Leonard chose to be included in his very early recording *Six Montreal Poets*.[6] Shortly after, it also appeared in his debut volume of poetry: *Let Us Compare Mythologies*.

"For Wilf and His House" is often mentioned to show how Leonard was attracted to imagery of Jesus. In the crucifixion, Leonard saw a poignant metaphor for much that both troubles and ennobles our human condition. In 1968, he insisted, "We have to rediscover the crucifixion. The crucifixion will again be understood as a universal symbol not just as an experiment in sadism or masochism or arrogance. It will have to be discovered 'cause that's where man is at. On the cross."[7] We again see this admiring yet outsider/spectator stance in the unnamed figure who witnesses the crucifixion in the poem "Ballad":

He pulled a flower
out of the moss
and struggled past soldiers
to stand at the cross.[8]

Artistic representations of the crucifixion naturally depict suffering, abandonment, and brokenness. Jesus's fate personified the societal violence that both repelled and so fascinated Leonard: "At the very centre of our culture," he said, "is a crucified man ...You have an image of violence at the very centre of our spiritual investigation."[9] At the same time, Christian artists have tended to portray in Jesus's face a peaceful acceptance of his fate, even transcendence. In a speech in 2011, Leonard said: "if one is to express the great inevitable defeat that awaits us all, it must be done within the strict confines of dignity and beauty."[10] Again and again in his life Leonard returned to these themes of gracefully accepting suffering. It's not hard to see the lines of continuity between "the lovely butterfly against the wood" and Leonard's life-long dedication to facing the crushing truths of life with dignity and beauty. Nicolet-Anderson writes: "Cohen works with biblical texts, thinks with biblical metaphors, in order to negotiate the chaos that for him defines the world."[11] In that sense, Jesus was a natural example for Leonard. Crucifixion shows the depths of human cruelty and brokenness. But there can be found in its receptions and depictions a nobility of brokenness that Leonard's work would also plumb. "The figure of Jesus is extremely attractive," said Leonard to journalist Robert O'Brian in 1987. "It's difficult not to fall in love with that person."[12]

Paul certainly would have agreed. That *Paul* was obsessed with Jesus might seem so obvious as to hardly be worth mentioning. But those who haven't dug deep into his letters may be surprised to realize that unlike Leonard, Paul is surprisingly *un*interested in Jesus of Nazareth, the man. For all Paul talks about Christ, he doesn't spend much time on Jesus the human being, whom he likely never met, although the two were roughly contemporaries. Paul never mentions Jesus's miracles or parables. He rarely alludes to biographical details about Jesus, or to Jesus's teachings known to us from the later gospels of Matthew, Mark, Luke, and John.[13] And he doesn't seem to know the compilation of Jesus's sayings, known as Q, that was probably circulating about the same time.

For him as with Leonard, the most important things about Jesus also tend to concern the end of Jesus's life. He says so explicitly:

> For I decided to know nothing among you except Jesus Christ,
> and him crucified ...
> None of the rulers of this age understood this [wisdom];
> for if they had, they would not have crucified the Lord of glory.[14]

Paul's words here are reminiscent of Leonard's, who in the following lines contrasts the Christ of faith with the earthly Jesus, all while maintaining the outsider's point of view mentioned earlier (yet ironically identifying with Christopher, the Jesus-bearing saint of ancient Christian myth):

> There is another Christopher
> Guide to Broken Ways
> Rejected Christ he carries far
> Yours he cannot raise.[15]

—

To better understand why Paul's letters don't contain details about the Jesus we know from the Christian gospels, a brief explanation might be helpful. In the Bible, the gospels appear before Paul's letters. Many people don't realize that this is not the order in which they were written. Paul composed a full generation, in some cases, two generations, before the gospels. His communications are the earliest New Testament documents.

The gospels were placed first in the volume known as the New Testament not because they're oldest, but because they deal with Jesus, the thematic centre of the collection. The gospels are persuasive biographies, meant to pass on the story and its significance. By contrast, Paul's letters were more like first-century emails. They're practical and arise from ad-hoc occasions. In them, Paul answers questions, checks up, admonishes certain people, greets and thanks others, and makes personal plans. Even though Paul's letters exhibit his thinking, even Romans (the most carefully worked-out) is not a theological treatise. None of Paul's letters are Jesus biographies, ancient or modern. Rather, Paul's letters are working documents.

This begs the question: if the gospels with their stories of Jesus are so important, why weren't they written earlier? Why wouldn't a biography of Jesus be written first? The answer is simple: biographies are written to preserve a heritage into a future. There is no need to do that if one doesn't believe there will *be* a future.

Paul and many other Christ followers of the first generation expected the coming reign of Israel's God, *in their lifetime* (I always tell my classes "next week, next month, the next couple of years, at the latest").[16] In Mark 9:1, Jesus says to his followers, "Truly I tell you, there are some standing here who will not taste death until they see that the kingdom of God has come with power." You do not need to write the story of Jesus for children and grandchildren you never expect to have. Paul – and other Jesus followers – believed Rome would soon be tossed out, the Caesars judged, idolators destroyed, and Israel vindicated. Paul even discouraged people from getting married and having children unless they absolutely couldn't help it, since to his mind there was little point.[17] Most of the small sect of Jesus followers initially believed that all the world would soon see the end of days and the return of their messiah, either to their judgment, or salvation.[18]

Given that expectation, it took decades after Paul for our oldest known gospel, the gospel of Mark, to be written. Its composition coincides with the deaths of the generation who knew Jesus personally. Christ wasn't returning within the presumed timeframe of their lifetimes. Communities started writing down the sayings and stories when they realized they could lose them. It is a reaction similar to the impulse we sometimes have to get our family histories from elderly parents or grandparents when we recognize they may soon be gone.

Unlike the gospels, which were meant for posterity, Paul's letters started as temporary, practical, and highly case-specific communications with some of the first generation of what later became Christianity.[19] Paul, in that first generation, seems to care little about Jesus's personal details. For Paul, what is important is not so much what Jesus did as what the God of Israel did *with* him – and what Paul also believed God would soon do *through* Jesus – that is, start the resurrection and trigger the judgment.[20] Paul downplays Jesus the man in favour of Christ the role, the catalyst of the Day of the Lord:

> Even though we once knew Christ from a human point of view,
> we know him no longer in that way.
> So if anyone is in Christ, there is a new creation:
> everything old has passed away;
> see, everything has become new![21]

On one major point, Leonard and Paul agree: Jesus encapsulates the human experience – a condition Leonard relished, and Paul yearned to escape. In what was likely his last surviving letter, Paul underlines our human solidarity with Jesus:

> Do you not know that all of us who have been baptized into
>   Christ Jesus
> Were baptized into his death?[22]
> For to me, living is Christ, and dying is gain.[23]

In "Show Me the Place," Leonard writes of a similar solidarity:

> Show me the place, help me roll away the stone;
> show me the place, I can't move this thing alone.
> Show me the place where the Word became a man.
> Show me the place where the suffering began.[24]

While Paul moves quickly from cross to resurrection, Leonard takes a longer path. In the gospels, and presumably for Paul, it is God or an angel who rolls away the stone on Easter morning. In Leonard's "Show Me the Place," it is the artist who must struggle with that task – and we never find out if it is successful. It is the act of *wrestling* with the stone, the calling out for help, that interests Leonard. If there is to be any resurrection, it must be wrestled out of its place.

In most of their writings, Paul's focus is on the divine action and Leonard's on the human condition. Put briefly: Paul is a preacher, Leonard a witness. Leonard's offering to the divine is to give suffering expression and dignity.[25] This doesn't mean his view of redemption is an incomplete version of Paul's. It is different – but with profound parallels, especially in the focus on human frailty and suffering. For Paul, human weakness is where a deeper divine wisdom can work. The world sees this as "foolishness."[26] I think Leonard agreed. In their own ways, both state that what human beings see and feel as abandonment is where God's work of redemption begins. For Leonard, the wrestling is the place where the divine presence is best recognized. Like Jacob who battled an angel all night long, the human task is to wrestle. Coming away from an encounter with the terrible transcendent alive, but limping, is the best one can hope for.[27]

Not triumphant and judging, but broken and on the cross, Jesus is presented by both as a pre-eminent example of where finite beings encounter the sacred and may find hope. However, for Leonard, love is never a victory march. Leonard is in no rush to give the man on "his lonely wooden tower" the kind of victory Paul ascribed to Jesus. Paul labours (with a resounding success over two millennia) to "spin" a humiliating execution into a triumph, and crucifixion as part of the divine plan all along. Leonard has no such motivation. He is always more interested in the raven than the dove,[28] and one suspects that his tendency to keep a bit of grit in every line would have made him especially uncomfortable with Paul's hymns of praise. Unlike Leonard, Paul tends to flip humiliation and exaltation. Exaltation is always the capstone to the latter's reflections on the crucified (and inevitably resurrected) Christ:

> Therefore God also highly exalted him
> and gave him the name
> that is above every name,
> so that at the name of Jesus

every knee should bend,
in heaven and on earth and under the earth,
and every tongue should confess
that Jesus Christ is Lord,
to the glory of God the Father.[29]

———

Several years after Cohen's death, I made a pilgrimage with my friend and fellow pilgrimage buff Stacey Engels.[30] We met at the former Zen centre, Leonard's house on Rue Vallières. Other visitors had left flowers and artwork taped to the brick, and a scrap of hand-written song lyrics had recently been stuck to a nearby lamppost. I had just purchased some clothing from J. Schreter's, the landmark St-Laurent store where Leonard often got his slippers. In the short moments we stood by the unmarked door of Cohen's house, other pilgrims gathered. Their accents from all over the world showed how widespread the poet's influence is. He may be gone, but as the four-storey mural of him on a nearby building attests, he is far from forgotten.

Stacey and I began to walk toward the Old Port, where the song "Suzanne" is set. As we meandered down Boulevard St-Laurent, we stopped at points here and there to reminisce about our own memories of life and events along the street, known as "La Main." Boulevard St-Laurent has gentrified, especially since the days when Leonard was growing up in Westmount and Irving Layton on the Plateau. But Leonard's trademark juxtapositions of saintly and sinful are still mirrored in Montreal. As Nicolet-Anderson points out, "it is down on the docks that spiritual and terrestrial meet and transform human life in a sacred space."[31] We ended our walk at the water, looking up at Our Lady of the Harbour, the statue above Notre-Dame-de-Bon-Secours Chapel, inspirational to the song "Suzanne."[32]

In the famous lines of "Suzanne," "Jesus was a sailor / When he walked upon the water / And he spent a long time watching / From his lonely wooden tower."[33] Leonard sets up Jesus as a saviour for the protagonist of the song: "and you want to travel with him, and you want to travel blind." Yet in the end, Jesus cannot help anyone, not even himself, because "he himself was broken."

The poem then passes Jesus over for the redemption held out by the woman for whom the song is named.[34] In the end, it is Suzanne who "takes your hand." She is the one whom you "know that you can trust," because "she's touched your perfect body with her mind." For Leonard, desire is the first stage (or perhaps more accurately, the precondition) for redemption. The sacred face of divine encounter is a human face that one longs for and comes to have faith in, whether the "half-crazy" Suzanne, or the "madness" in the broken face on the cross.[35]

In their respective writings, Leonard and Paul both spend time at the cross. Not surprisingly, however, they part ways on Easter. For Paul, the message was that God took Jesus, seemingly abandoned and forsaken, and raised him from the dead, confirming him as the messiah and the first-born of the general resurrection to come.[36] Paul does indeed focus on the crucifixion, but he always includes the resurrection in that thinking. Leonard's lyrics share the focus on the divine presence – even in abandonment – but his lyrics linger there. He is not interested in exaltation. His salvation is experienced in the limited, the finite, and in seeking out a safe haven where something beautiful can, perhaps, be born.[37] Especially for the young Leonard, if there was a messianic task, it was in an act of redemption performed as a kind of alchemy by the artist himself.[38]

Paul's view of Jesus is what theologians call "Christological," meaning focused on Jesus as divinized messiah rather than as earthly, crucified, teacher.[39] Despite Paul's obsession with the cross, he inevitably ends with the resurrection and the coming Day of the Lord. Very soon, as Paul writes, Jesus will:

reign until he has put all his enemies under his feet.
The last enemy to be destroyed is death ...
When all things are subjected to him,
then the Son himself will also be subjected to the one ...
so that God may be all in all.[40]

In certain poems – "Closing Time," "Beside the Shepherd" – Leonard also alludes to this catastrophic, history-ending event sometimes known as the Day of the Lord. It may surprise Cohen fans that these two share this image in common from their Jewish scriptures.[41] But on the question of whether to expect *Jesus* on that day of Jewish expectation, Leonard and Paul differ. Leonard sticks to the incarnation, the mystery that Jesus was born, lived, suffered, and died as a human being, like the rest of us. Or perhaps it would be truer to the poet to express it the other way around:[42] for Leonard, we poor human beings are born to live, suffer, and die in hope of grace and resurrection, just as Jesus did.

TEXT MEDITATION

Listen to: "Suzanne," *Songs of Leonard Cohen* (1967).

On the role of Jesus in a typology of redemption, compare:

And you want to travel with him
you want to travel blind
and you think maybe you'll trust him
for he's touched your perfect body
with his mind
            ("Suzanne," *Stranger Music,* 95–6)

For if we have been united with him in a death like [Jesus's],
we will certainly be united with him in a resurrection like his.
We know that our old self was crucified with him
so that the body of sin might be destroyed, and we might
    no longer
be enslaved to sin. For whoever has died is free from sin.
But if we have died with Christ, we believe we will also live
    with him.
    (Romans 6:5-8)

FURTHER READING

I highly recommend Nicolet-Anderson's "Leonard Cohen's Use of the Bible." It provides good background reading not only for this chapter but also for chapter 10, "Come Healing."

For a different take on "Suzanne" and its relationship to the Bible (and a much more extensive treatment of the "walking on water" connections), see O'Neil, "Leonard Cohen, Singer of the Bible."

4 Death of a Ladies' Man

Leonard, Paul, and Women

It takes some audacity to claim that Leonard Cohen and St Paul have anything in common in terms of their relations to women. But I would like to try! This chapter's argument is simple: Leonard often expressed his intimacy with the divine in terms of his loving women sexually.[1] Paul often expressed his intimacy with women in terms of his non-sexual love of God. Whether getting closer to God through sexual connection or getting closer to God through promoting sexual abstinence in hopes of a final transcendence of gender (a subject to which Leonard also referred), the issue for both Leonard and Paul was always God.

Interestingly, a side-effect was that each was surrounded by women. Both Leonard and Paul had significant female business partners, patrons,[2] and mentors. These people played crucial roles in their lives. Jennifer Warnes's tribute album to Leonard, for instance, worked symbiotically to improve both their careers.[3] Other important female collaborators included Sharon Robinson and Anjani Thomas. As for Paul, in Romans 16:7 where he is seeking support, he makes sure to list the names of many women as apostles and colleagues, some of whom were evidently his superiors in a movement he had joined later than they had.

While Leonard slept with many of his patrons and collaborators, Paul most emphatically did not. Oddly enough, this celibacy did not mean that his writings show less connection to the real lives of women than do Leonard's. However real and active women may have been in Leonard's life, in his lyrics they are often treated as objects. In his oeuvres, women are often presented as metaphors, as mechanisms used to "think with," compose with, or otherwise benefit from.[4] Lévi-Strauss's term "good to think with" is handy shorthand for referring to occasions in which male authors use female characters for examining male-centred issues.[5] "I never met a woman until I was sixty-five," Leonard once remarked: "Instead, I saw all kinds of miracles in front of me."[6] The heteronormative male artist's gaze is central to such an observation.

Leonard employs women as props and object lessons in his lyrics far more than does Paul. Paul's letters (and it's important to specify here that we are talking about his seven authentic letters) are full of women prophesying, providing financial support and leadership for the movement, and carrying his words to other cities. In other words, Leonard's women tend to be tropes, and Paul's women real-life, named, and actual persons. Ironically, the ancient man, from an even more patriarchal society, writes with more awareness of the real person than does the modern. Some of this is no doubt due to Paul's eschatological frame of focus. He believed that all human differences, including gender, would soon be levelled by the God of Israel's takeover of society, and his task was, in part at least, to try to reflect those changes in the moment. At the same time, he could not escape his social context entirely. Even while relying on the substantial help of his female patrons in the movement, he was focussed on men to the point of writing at least one entire letter – Galatians, and possibly 1 Thessalonians – almost exclusively for them.[7]

Leonard famously courted younger women – often much younger. Beautiful and desirable women are the objectified vehicles through which the male poet experiences a beautiful, desirable, divine.[8]

G-d opened my eyes this morning
Loosened the bands of sleep
Let me see the waitress's tiny earrings

And the merest foothills
Of her small breasts[9]

Especially in the first of his surviving letters to the Corinthians, Paul exhibits a concern for the needs and "anxieties" of domestic life, and an awareness of the mutuality of the marriage bond, that is highly unusual in the first-century Roman world. Limited as it is, this awareness of mutuality likely originates from his Judaism.[10] However, even here, Paul's message concerning celibacy is predicated on valuing the kind of self-control that the ancient world attributed to the "male" domain. That is, women become more "equal" for Paul and other ancients as they become more *like* men.

Even casual Cohen fans know there's no shortage of material when it comes to Leonard and women. Leonard was as quick as anyone, usually quicker, to point out the obsession:

It's not that I like
To live in a hotel
In a place like India
And write about G-d
And run after women
It seems to be
What I do[11]

Leonard presents his attractions to both God and women as natural, although there is more than a whiff of anxiety in his descriptions of both. Meanwhile, he typically cultivated and narrated those attractions with an eye to his artistic output. Christophe Lebold writes that Leonard's work consisted of his "ceaseless construction and deconstruction of himself as Great Lover of women and God."[12] Inevitably, when "woman" is an ideal, and women are placed on pedestals, their real personhood is kept at a distance. Whatever his private feelings, this objectification happens in many, perhaps most of

Leonard's works, at least before his final albums. The playful fusion of spirituality and eroticism is his trademark.[13] Sex, love, and desire are constant themes from the first collection of his poetry, released in his early twenties, to his almost thankful pronouncement of relief – "I don't need a lover / The wretched beast is tame" – in his last album, released just seventeen days before his death.[14]

———

These three themes – sex, love, and desire – must be disentangled to understand the nuances of Leonard's relationships to women.

Firstly, god-language is a handy device for talking about sex. In poems like "Thing,"[15] or "So Long, Marianne,"[16] using the language of prayer or worship for sex allows Leonard to describe in elevated and sacred language what might otherwise sound crass, furtive, illicit, or simply banal.[17] But there was also an overlap of intention and place for Leonard: a woman's body was a shrine (although notably, not her thoughts).[18] For the poet of the sacred imperfect, the boundary between sacred and profane is intentionally ambiguous. Lebold notes how Columbia Records' early strategy with Leonard was to portray him as the "expert decoder of the female mystery."[19] When he sings "I've heard there was a secret chord, that David played to please the Lord,"[20] it might be a one-four-five progression, and it might be a reference to ancient Israel's most famous king. But the secret chord might also be an allusion to how an attentive man can best please a woman. And Leonard, at least in his poetry and public persona, was nothing if not attentive. Lebold calls Cohen "gynophiliac."[21] References to oral sex abound in Leonard's works.

For Leonard, part of the secret was to identify desire as the common element in both worship and in sexual love[22] – but not necessarily in the final achievement of transcendence. Desire defines the artist. It also creates the art. But love stands above desire and brings with it a peace unavailable to the seeker. Perhaps it would be more accurate of

Leonard's poetry to identify how love begins in desire but eventually moves beyond it (much as he worked to maintain ongoing friendships with his long list of former lovers). Interestingly, this can become an almost ascetic valuation of love, which again has a parallel in Paul's writing. For example, in his famous "love chapter" of 1 Corinthians 13, the apostle talks about the ineffability of love and how it will only fully be known after this world is no more.

In his lyrics, Leonard tends to pass over the word "desire" for the more overtly religious and ambiguous term "longing." The Hebrew Bible contains several Psalms of longing.[23] One of Leonard's volumes of poetry is even entitled *Book of Longing*. He suggests that it is only when longing is quieted that real love can take its place. The "come healing of the body / come healing of the mind"[24] prayer was part of aging that he seemed to welcome. It was also part of his ascetic practice that we'll talk about in a future chapter: a yearning for transcendence expressed throughout his work.

———

Leonard came by his attention to women naturally. He lost his father at the age of nine and grew up mentored by important female figures. One of the chapters of Simmons's biography is titled "House of Women."[25] Johanna Schneller simply points to what she calls Leonard's "mother issues."[26] Leonard likely would have agreed:

> The last time that I saw him
> he was trying hard to get
> a woman's education
> but he's not a woman yet[27]

We simply don't know about Paul's early relationships to women. But we can say with confidence that women played an important role in the apostle's *later* life. As with the rest of his biography, the evidence is scattered. But it's there. In Paul's letter to the assembly in Philippi, for example, he mentions only five individuals, three of whom are women. Two of these women, Euodia and Syntyche, he says, "have struggled beside me in the work of the gospel."[28] "Beside me" is important. The two are clearly community leaders.

At the end of his letter to the Christ-assembly in Rome, Paul does something that ancient letter-writers often did: he greets specific individuals. This was the ancient equivalent of "Say hi to your family from me," but with heightened stakes due to ancient codes of honour and patronage. To greet certain people in such a formal letter usually meant that those persons might guarantee a good reception for the communication. In other words, Paul mentions these individuals, many of them women, because they were "status" people for both the sender and the recipients.

Romans is the only surviving letter of Paul's to a Christ-assembly he himself did not initiate. Paul needed help. It is very possible that Romans, which is the most serene and careful of his works, was written as a form of "spin control" after his passionate, and unfortunate, communication with the Galatians.[29] Paul was anxious for the support of the Roman Jesus-followers. Women seemed to be among his greatest supporters, and the crucial lynchpins of power dynamics whom he hoped would help him and his cause.

The last chapter of Romans contains Paul's greetings to twenty-nine people. Remarkably, about a third of the individuals are women. It's especially intriguing that more women than men are linked by Paul to "the work of the gospel." Moreover, the two people he commends at the outset are both women, suggesting that they were his most influential contacts. The first, Phoebe, was a "minister" in Cenchreae (near Corinth) and also the person who carried and performed the letter for Paul, explaining its contents to the recipients. This meant she had the means and status to be able to travel:

Welcome her in the Lord as is fitting for the saints,
And help her in whatever she may require of you,
For she has been a benefactor of many and of myself as well.[30]

The word "benefactor" has been variously translated in English Bibles in ways that hide its import. In Greek it is the word for "patron" (implying a financial backer and lender of honour to an endeavour). Its frequent translation into terms like "helper" diminishes Phoebe's obvious monetary and social clout, and is misleading. In much the same way as the importance of women such as Anjani Thomas and Jennifer Warnes might be passed over by the more inattentive of Leonard's fans (although not by Leonard), it is in the *reception* of Paul that the importance of Paul's female patrons and collaborators has suffered.

Immediately after the passage mentioned above, Paul's first greeting is to "Prisca and Aquila, who work with me." Prisca is a woman's name. In the rigidly patriarchal Roman society of the day, it was rare in such correspondence for a wife's name to be listed first, before her husband's. Naming Prisca implies a hierarchy of importance. Paul goes on to say that they "risked their necks" for him. Almost immediately after this, he greets a woman named Mary, and another named Junia. He says about Junia that she was in prison with him, and that she and Andronicus are "prominent among the apostles, and they were in Christ before I was."[31]

Paul acknowledged – in fact, he's quick to point out – that these women were not only his equals, but also his mentors and superiors. He accepts without hesitation that women were as likely to preach as he was ("prominent among the apostles"). He calls them ministers in the assemblies, although he does promote gendered dress codes while ministering.[32] All this leadership by women seems somewhat revolutionary given later Christian patriarchy. It is explained, in part, by the fact that Paul and other early apostles likely inherited a limited gender-egalitarianism from Jesus himself,[33] from their shared apocalyptic Jewish context, and from their eschatological hopes.

So then: why did Paul end up with his reputation as a woman-hater? The short answer is: there are *other* texts attributed to Paul in the New Testament; texts reflecting much more conservative Roman views about women and their "place." Despite their authorship traditions, the letters of 1 and 2 Timothy, and Titus, traditionally called "Pastoral letters," show every sign of being written long after Paul had died. Their views about woman and sexuality in general could not be more diametrically opposed to Paul's. These later letters contain passages that have been used throughout Christian history and Western culture to argue for women's subservience and inferiority:

> Let a woman learn in silence with full submission.
> I permit no woman to teach or to have authority over a man;
>   she is to keep silent.
> For Adam was formed first, then Eve; and Adam was not
>   deceived,
> But the woman was deceived and became a transgressor.
> Yet she will be saved through childbearing.[34]

How can the same person write the last lines of Romans, where he greets important women leaders and appeals for help to women apostles, and writes instructions for what women should wear while leading worship and prophesying ... and then write that women are "to keep silent"? How can the same person write so eloquently and passionately on salvation coming through unearned gracefulness, and then write that for women, it will come "through childbearing"? It seems impossible.

That's probably because it is.[35] Historians of early Christianity overwhelmingly conclude that in fact Paul did *not* write 1 and 2 Timothy and Titus; a strong majority of scholars conclude the same about Ephesians and Colossians, in which verses commanding wives to "submit to" husbands occur. The historians look at many factors in making this decision, but here I highlight three: the later letters' attitudes toward women and sex (they have lost Paul's ambivalence about marriage and his celebration of celibacy); their lack of urgency about the end of the world (they have lost Paul's idea that Christ's return is immanent); and finally, their hierarchical ideas about church structure (in a "last-days" movement like Paul's, organization is usually more temporary, fluid, and charismatic. Sustainable institutional guidelines and structures are hardly a concern).[36] What's more, when you compare the specific vocabulary of 1 and 2 Timothy and Titus, Ephesians, and Colossians – that is, the Greek words and style they use – to letters like Romans on the one hand, and on the other, to documents from a century later, the strong similarity of the disputed epistles to the latter makes this conclusion even stronger.[37]

Most scholars believe the Pastoral letters with their denunciations of women, in addition to the "disputed" letters of Ephesians and Colossians with their endorsement of hierarchically structured marriage, were written as much as fifty years after Paul's martyrdom under Nero. That is: *these letters were penned in Paul's name, but not by Paul.* Such pseudepigraphal attribution was not uncommon in the Greek and early Roman periods. It can be seen in books like 1 Enoch, The Testament of Abraham, 2 Baruch, The Gospel of Mary, or The Gospel of Peter. The pseudonymous letters, borrowing authority by using the name of Paul, show signs that the young Jesus movement had resigned itself to the fact that Jesus had not returned immediately as hoped, and had begun to accommodate itself to wider Roman society. This would have been true especially after the Jewish Revolt against Rome in the late 60s resulted in suspicion against Jewish groups. The subservience to which these letters tried to force women in the movement was typical of "respectable" Roman circles. It was also typical of a Jewish movement that was rapidly transforming into a majority non-Jewish membership and was trying to divorce itself from its Jewish roots.

In very different ways, both Leonard and Paul began life during a time of conservative, "family values" retrenchment. Leonard grew up in the early 1950s. At that time, women were being pushed out of the public spheres and the professions they had held during the Second World War. 1950s advertising told women, not so subtly, that now that the men were back from the war, their job was to stay home.[38] Perhaps partly due to the independence and influence of his own mother Micha, whose flamboyance and dramatic nature[39] made her stand out, Leonard was part of the 1960s reaction to those restrictions. Paul grew up in a post-Augustan world where, at the direction of the very highest ranks of Roman society, women likewise were being increasingly restricted and moved out of the public sphere.[40] Paul found himself part of a "last-days" movement that looked back to the women around Jesus, and also reacted against such restrictions.

The *real* Paul, the Paul who dictated Romans and Philippians, worked closely with women. But where Leonard fetishized sex, equating it with worship, Paul did the opposite. In 1 Corinthians 7:7, Paul exclaims, "I wish everyone could be [celibate] like I am!" Of course, deliberate abstention from sex is also a kind of fetishization and a preoccupation with it.

It seems likely that part of the reason Paul could work so well with women against some of the more restrictive gender norms of his day was that he believed both he and they were in some sense beyond gender, and certainly beyond sexual desire. Paul famously writes that "there is no longer male and female; for all of you are one in Christ Jesus."[41] Compare this idea of gender-dissolution with the artwork for Leonard's 1974 album *New Skin for the Old Ceremony*; it features a woodcut depicting the *coniunctio spirituum*, the union of the male-female principle. Freedman points out connections here to the Kabbalah, "which stresses the mystical essentiality of sex; the conjunction of male and female anticipates the mystical union of the human and the divine."[42] Where Paul wants to transcend gender and attraction, Leonard highlights the physical coming together of male and female as the site of the highest spiritual union. Just as it's hard to imagine Leonard's work without a sexual component, it's hard to imagine Paul's *with* one. But both these supposed opposites are true for similar reasons. It all comes back to God.

In Paul's day and to the present, Judaism holds a healthy place for sex both for procreation and specifically for pleasure (including women's pleasure).[43] This made Paul an outlier when he teaches in his letters that sex and marriage should, if at all possible, be avoided. What for Leonard and most of Judaism was almost sacramental was, for Paul, a distraction from divine communion:

I want you to be free from anxieties.
The unmarried man is anxious about the affairs of the Lord;
how to please the Lord;
But the married man is anxious about the affairs of the world,
How to please his wife, and his interests are divided ... [likewise]
The married woman is anxious about the affairs of the world,
How to please her husband.[44]

Reading such words today, we need to keep in mind that Paul was part of a minority stream within Judaism. Some late second-temple apocalyptic Jews really believed a messiah would arrive soon (next week, next month, in the next few years at the latest). Despite some change in his thinking over the course of his letters, Paul's advice was consistently given in and for that particular moment when, with one eye on the cosmic clock, he counted down to the Day of the Lord. In that soon-to-be-moment, there would be no ethnic differences, no enslavement, and perhaps no marriage.[45] For that reason, in 1 Corinthians Paul advised Jesus-following slaves to obtain their freedom only if they could easily do so. After all, they would soon be free anyway. His advice for married couples in the Corinthian assembly was to abstain from sex occasionally to better focus on prayer (an ascetic practice), but to do so only for mutually agreed times, being sure to come together again periodically to fulfill mutual conjugal duties.[46] To young couples, he advised not getting married unless they couldn't control their sexual urges, which he allowed would be difficult. It seems that Paul believed that in the coming Realm of God there would be no sex, perhaps even no gender.[47] One wonders what Paul would have made of Leonard's quest for the sacred through bodily pleasure!

In the end, we return to the observation that whatever women's real-world practical contributions to their lives and work may have been, they are described in the writings of Leonard and Paul from a male point of view. Leonard rhapsodizes women as muses, obstacles to art, distractions, or channels of the divine, but rarely as human beings. Paul seems to grant more agency to women, but the language he uses generally acknowledges them only for the "manly" characteristics they share with himself as benefactors, mediators, those who are working hard and risking their necks.[48] For both writers, the place of women is solidly within a discourse about masculinity.

TEXT MEDITATION

Listen to: "Death of a Ladies' Man," *Death of a Ladies' Man* (1977).

Compare the views of women contained in the following passages:

> Now the master of this landscape
> he was standing at the view
> with a sparrow of St. Francis
> that he was preaching to.
> She beckoned to the sentry
> of his high religious mood.
> She said, "I'll make a space between my legs,
> I'll teach you solitude."
>   ("Death of a Ladies' Man," *Stranger Music*, 227)

Greet Prisca and Aquila, who work with me in Christ Jesus,
and who risked their necks for my life, to whom not only I
 give thanks,
but all the churches of the Gentiles. Greet also the church in
 their house.
… Greet Mary, who has worked very hard among you.
Greet Andronicus and Junia, my relatives who were in prison
 with me;
They are prominent among the apostles, and they were in
 Christ before I was.

 (Romans 16:3–7)

FURTHER READING

For more on the themes raised by this chapter, there is no better
general resource than Parks, Sheinfeld, and Warren, *Jewish and
Christian Women in the Ancient Mediterranean*. The entire book is useful
to students of the ancient world, but for this chapter please consult
especially pages 161–3 "Women Followers of Jesus in Paul."

The phrase "using women to think with" describes how male authors, including Leonard and Paul, have used women as types rather
than real people in their writings. More on this can be found in Parks,
Sheinfeld, and Warren, page 222.

For more on Leonard Cohen's relationships with women, in addition to Simmons's biography see Lebold, "From Existential Troubadour to Crooner of Light" and Schneller, "Cohen's Tales of Seduction
Look Different through a #MeToo Lens."

Some readers may find the idea that Paul only wrote seven of the
letters attributed to him shocking. A good place to begin exploring
more on this subject is in articles on the website *Bible Odyssey*. See,
for example, Concannon, "Paul and Authorship" and Eastman, "The
Pastoral Epistles."

5 Traveling Light

Comparing Leonard and Paul's relationships to women was a daunting task. Perhaps even more daunting is to suggest the two were ascetics. Yet I am indeed proposing that each in his own way was a practitioner of asceticism.

Cohen fans may respond: Paul, maybe. But what about the Courvoisier Leonard carried in his pocket?[1] What about the sex and drugs? What about "we were running for the money and the flesh," in the Chelsea Hotel with Janis Joplin and limousines waiting on the street?[2] Certainly, Leonard was no stranger to the high life. He often introduced his concerts by saying that to handle his depression he tried everything: "hashish, speed, cocaine, alcohol, tobacco, and other drugs."[3] Yet for certain periods of their lives, both individuals merit consideration as ascetics.

It partly comes down to definition.

Firstly, there is the question of whether asceticism is only a refraining *from*, or if it also entails a taking *on* of something: a discipline, for example, or a practice. If asceticism is simply renunciation, must it be renunciation accompanied by intention or purpose? Elizabeth Castelli writes that "asceticism is frequently distinguished from other behavior, whether religious or not, by its unsettling and often extreme difference – its refusal of the ordinary, the contingent, the quotidian."[4] Most of us who even temporarily take on some mild form of renunciatory behaviour do so to disturb our routines, often in hopes of a more permanent change or result. Some hope to contribute to a personal or societal transformation. Examples might include fasting to experience greater gratitude or humility, refraining from social media in order to gain contemplative perspective, or boycotting sensationalism and oversimplification of issues.

Then there is the relationship between ascetic practice and desire. As a non-coffee drinker, I can hardly claim any virtue from refraining from the drink – I never started the habit in the first place. Is it renunciation if it takes no effort? Like the sixth-century Irish monks who reportedly left their beloved homeland weeping, part of asceticism's worth is surely found in giving up precisely that which we most want.

If asceticism means the intentional denial of worldly pleasures in pursuit of transcendent good, that doesn't sound like certain periods of Leonard's life. But it does sound like others. At the age of sixty, after what was already a decades-long association with Kyozan Joshu Roshi and Zen Buddhism, Leonard took up the monk's life. He became a resident at the Zen Centre at Mount Baldy, in the high mountains not far from Los Angeles. Mount Baldy is a place for the most extreme forms of self-discipline.

> Alarm awakened me at 2:30 a.m.:
> got into my robes
> *kimono* and *hakama*[5]

The Mount Baldy centre is anything but fancy. It consists of an abandoned Boy Scout camp, complete with dilapidated cabins, 6,500 feet above sea level in the San Gabriel mountains. There monks sit for hours in meditation, often in severe physical pain. Weaker monks are weeded out by physical testing. Immobility is part of the discipline: while meditating, if you must blow your nose, it runs down your face. If you have to urinate, and the *jikijitsu* (the monk or nun in charge of the zendo, or meditation hall) does not say the sitting is over, you do so where you sit. Intense pain, prolonged sleep deprivation, extreme cold in winter, a crushingly sparse caloric intake – Mount Baldy is boot-camp for Buddhists.[6] It was there that Leonard put in his time, "shivering," as he puts it, "on the altar of enlightenment."[7] During some parts of his life, Leonard was practically the opposite of abstemious. He was hedonistic, perhaps, and certainly self-advertised as sensuous, and carnal. But for a significant portion of his later life, he could also be described as monastic.

Once more we must note that, for Leonard, his association with Buddhism was in no way a denial of his Judaism. Zen Buddhism is not a teaching so much as a physical practice. "I have a perfectly good religion," said Leonard, when asked about it. Simmons reports him as pointing out that "Roshi had never made any attempt to give him a new one."[8] Leonard's piece "My Teacher" ends with the words "When he was certain that I was incapable of self-reform, he flung me across the fence of the Torah."[9]

Picking up on the themes of last chapter, asceticism is commonly understood to be the antithesis of desire. But perhaps it would be more accurate to propose that asceticism is a *redirection* of desire. In its very denial of the body, ascetic impulse emphasizes it. Paul claims to have overcome bodily needs, as does Leonard; but while Leonard's lyrics celebrate the body, Paul's words generally do not.[10]

Leonard seemed to try to use asceticism to transmute his burden of sexual desire into longing for the divine. He wanted to explore how his worship of God might be expressed beyond his obsession with women, and how the (to that point) rather useful attachments that characterized his poetry might fit with Zen Buddhism's philosophy of non-attachment and emptiness. The mash-up of all these seemingly disparate elements, including addiction, sometimes finds expression in his verse:

> The Lord is such a monkey
> He's such a woman too
> Such a place of nothing
> Such a face of you.[11]

For both writers, individual asceticism was part of a larger social movement. Leonard was part of the 1960s sexual revolution. However authentic his Buddhism, he was also part of a well-documented mid-century turn by younger North Americans to Eastern religiosity.[12] Paul was part of a sexual revolution as well, an increasingly-understood turn toward celibacy within first-century BCE and first-century CE Judaism.[13] Both revolutions were against the perceived social norms of their day – Leonard's against the puritanism and formal religiosity of the 1950s, and Paul's against the libertinism he and many other Jews felt was rampant in idolatrous Roman society.[14]

Paul made it abundantly clear that he was a sexual ascetic. In his letter to the Christ-followers at Corinth he quotes one of their sayings approvingly: "It is well for a man not to touch a woman."[15] Unlike Leonard, this is advice Paul knows he is already following. He makes it sound easy: "I wish that all were [celibate] as I myself am. But each has a particular gift from God."[16]

Leonard at times seems serious about sexual renunciation,[17] but he also jokes about it:

O, I had such a wonderful dream, she said.
I dreamed you made love to me.
At last, he said to himself, the spirit
has taken up some of the heavy work.[18]

Ascetic practice isn't just about sex, of course, although celibacy usually gets highest billing. Even in his young, seemingly carefree days, when he cultivated the appearance of a partygoer, Leonard's writing schedule was extremely disciplined. He would rise early, eat simply, and write for hours. Paul's letters likewise touch on other aspects of what we could call asceticism, particularly its self-discipline:

Athletes exercise self-control in all things;
they do it to receive a perishable wreath, but we an imperishable one.
So I do not run aimlessly, nor do I box as though beating the air;
But I punish my body and enslave it,
so that after proclaiming to others I should not be disqualified.[19]

The term "disqualified" is part of Paul's athletic metaphor. But he must have meant it also as a very real possibility concerning his status on the coming Day of the Lord. Asceticism, for Paul, was a defense against being declared unworthy by the divine judge:

For his [Christ's] sake I have suffered the loss of all things,
and I regard them as rubbish,
in order that I may gain Christ.[20]

Paul makes it sound like his call cost him dearly. Yet he states that whatever price he paid socially and physically is for him part of his spiritual discipline. He seems to have considered his various physical hardships, including imprisonment, shipwreck, beatings, and involuntary starvation, as part of his ascetic practice.[21] Surprisingly, in his surviving letters Paul never mentions fasting as such. However, given the fact that Jesus almost certainly fasted like other ancient Jews before him,[22] and that fasting was a part of the practice of many early Christians immediately after Paul, it's hard to believe that this spiritual discipline would have somehow skipped the link in the chain that included the historical (Jewish) Paul.[23]

Fasting was definitely a life-long practice for Leonard. Already at the age of twenty-three or twenty-four, his archives show that he was taking books about fasting out of the library. His early interest may have been with an eye to the stage. Combatting what Simmons calls a familial tendency to roundness, Leonard strove to maintain the angular facial features for which he became iconic. According to his biographer, Leonard's fasting combined the spiritual and the practical. "Fasting focused his mind for writing," she notes, "but there was vanity in it also; it kept his body thin and his face gaunt and serious."[24] In his own work, Leonard ascribed the practice to more devout motives: "As soon as I understood (even to a limited degree) that this is G-d's world I began to lose weight immediately."[25] And again:

> I'm fasting secretly
> to make my face thin
> so G-d can love me[26]

Despite his fasting, the food issues Paul addresses in his surviving letters have more to do with being the self-proclaimed apostle to the non-Jews. As such he had other, kosher, fish to fry. In several of his letters, Paul deals with the sticky problem of how non-Jewish Jesus followers and Jewish Jesus followers could eat together. Not only was kashrut (kosherness) a factor, so was the fact that meat in the ancient world almost inevitably came to the markets via temple sacrifice. There, before butchering, it had normally first been offered to a local god. This was a definite no-no for many Jews. In the ancient world, as today, Jews often chose vegetarianism as the simplest solution for how to follow kosher in a non-kosher culture (almost twenty centuries later, Leonard sometimes did the same). But Paul had to convince *non-Jewish* Jesus followers, some of whom to that point had quite happily combined their non-kosher diets with involvement in local synagogues, that in light of the imminent judgment this should now be a consideration for them as well. Passages from his letters show how he tried to negotiate this tricky social issue.[27]

At first glance, Leonard's asceticism seems much more personal than Paul's. In 1988 he said: "I've always needed a room, a table, and a chair and I don't like to have much more than that in them."[28] On Saturday nights in his lonely cabin on Mt Baldy, Leonard fought to control his demons and resist his self-documented desires. By contrast, from his prison cells in Philippi and Rome, Paul foresaw and welcomed the end of *all* demons, all "powers and dominions," even death itself.

However, a closer look at Leonard and Paul breaks down any distinction between personal and corporate. Both saw their personal asceticism as supporting their public message.

Leonard's lyrics frequently mourn societal evil – the murder and rape that go hand in hand with the attachments our world has for power.[29] Although he would have attributed it more to divine agency, Paul too believed that personal asceticism led the way to a more just communal future.

However, it is important to remember that despite their cultures being so different, both writers were free, educated, urban, and male, privileged in various ways by their respective societies. We will turn in the next chapter to what their masculinity might have meant to each of them. Certainly, for each man, asceticism or renunciation meant something very different from the experiences of the enslaved, the women, and the other-gendered around them who could not give up something that was never theirs in the first place. In the ancient world, as in ours, what some see as asceticism is simply, for others, daily life.[30]

TEXT MEDITATION

Listen to: "Traveling Light," *You Want It Darker* (2016).

Compare the views of asceticism expressed in the following:

I don't smoke no cigarette
I don't drink no alcohol
I ain't had much loving yet
But that's always been your call
Hey I don't miss it baby
I got no taste for anything at all
      (Cohen, "Darkness," *The Flame*, 113)

"All things are lawful for me," but not all things are beneficial.
"All things are lawful for me," but I will not be dominated by
    anything.
"Food is meant for the stomach and the stomach for food,"
and God will destroy both one and the other.

    (1 Corinthians 6:12–14)

FURTHER READING

For more reading on Cohen as an ascetic, see Grayston, "Monastic in His Own Way: Thomas Merton and Leonard Cohen." Mus's and Trehearne's excellent resource on Cohen is titled *The Demons of Leonard Cohen*. You will find sections in this book on Leonard's asceticism, and much more. It is a treasure for Cohen fans and scholars.

For more on Paul's asceticism, and asceticism's relationship to the New Testament, see the essays in Vaage and Wimbush, eds, *Asceticism and the New Testament*. On how the ascetic impulse in early Christianity and early Judaism affected women and enabled their leadership, see Parks, Sheinfeld, and Warren, *Jewish and Christian Women*, pages 288–92.

6 I'm Your Man

Leonard and Paul's Masculinity

I have talked about the importance in their lives and careers of Leonard and Paul's attitudes to women. If I failed at the same time to point out how being socialized into masculinity influenced their work, or how *everyone* has gender, we would be missing a significant piece of how these two showed themselves to their worlds. Leonard and Paul were men in cultures where that label was important. It was also important specifically to *them*. However, that importance did not have the same repercussions in each time and society. "Act like men"[1] could and did mean something different in the first century than the twenty-first.

In the same way that ideals of femininity exert pressures, ideals of masculinity also weighed – and still weigh – heavily. Each of these writers upheld masculine expectations of their time in some ways, and subverted them (or at least presented themselves as subverting them) in others.[2] The attitudes of both to powerful women betray a kind of anxiety that says more about conflicted masculinities than it does about the women they discuss.[3] For that reason, it is impossible to talk about Leonard and Paul's attitudes toward women or their asceticism without touching on their historical contexts, their own situatedness within gendered norms, and what their respective societies defined as masculinity.

On the one hand, each lived in what we might call "Hollywood cowboy" cultures. That is, both lived in societies allergic to male sensitivity and vulnerability. Two thousand years of differences mask some stark continuities: in 1960s movie posters, James Bond stands with a phallic-looking pistol over a half-naked prostrate woman. In first-century coins, a Roman soldier stands over a half-naked prostrate woman with his phallically-positioned sword.[4] In both periods, masculinity is established through bravado, exercised in domination, and proven by stoic (ascetic) self-control, especially during times of hardship.

In Paul's day, masculinity was defined simply but effectively as power. Only the most elite attained that status.[5] The Roman social pyramid was steep, with very few at its top. Power over others and over oneself was supremely manly, and as such there were very few people (no matter their gender) who measured up to being a true man, for which the ancient Romans used the term "vir."[6] Aristotle and Galen were among the first to define gender in terms of a single category of elite men – and everyone else who failed to live up to them.

Paul's society would have thought of not only women, but also enslaved men, "barbarian" peoples, and anyone with a physical disability or intellectual challenges as incomplete men. For our purposes at least, it is not too much of an oversimplification to say that for Romans, there was only one gender, the Roman male or "vir." Everyone else fit somewhere on the ladder leading to that apex of performance.

Of course, the ancients understood and delighted in sexual difference. However, in Greek and Roman societies, masculinity and femininity were not first and foremost a function of biology. They were a spectrum, one end of which implied failure and weakness (femininity) and the other end of which implied nobility and triumph (masculinity). The "positive" end of the gender spectrum was attained through noble behaviour and the public exercise of power.[7] The vast majority of people born male were not considered full "men." Women, along with male and female slaves and most non-citizens, were unable to achieve the status of a Roman vir not because of their physiology, but because of their "weak" behaviour or their lack of power or agency over others. This was a lack Paul would have been seen by many to share. Once you begin looking for it, it's impossible not to see how his awareness of his lesser standing comes out in his writing.[8]

The Middle Stoicism of Cicero and Seneca popular in Paul's day (and woven into his letters) found a way around this; it redefined manliness by saying that even though most people have little power, you can still be noble and manly if you master that over which you do have power, namely yourself. Several ancient texts refer to women or elderly men as "manly" precisely for their displays of self-control. For instance, 2 Maccabees 7:21 describes the Jewish woman who stood up to a tyrant as "filled with a noble spirit" and having "a man's courage," and 4 Maccabees 15:30 calls her "more noble than males in endurance, more manly than men in resistance." Mygdonia, Maximilla, and Thecla are all apocryphal Christian women who were reported to have "become" male, even in appearance, due to acts of self-control, nobility, and bravery (see the *Acts of Thomas, Acts of Andrew*, and *Acts of Paul and Thecla*).

Leonard, on the other hand, *depended* for the success of his writing on a specifically two-gender binary, emphasized even while he longed for union with the female "other." In many of his writings, the male/female relationship is caricatured as one of conquest, or of hunter and hunted, with the male inevitably the hunter.[9] "Any man over 30 knows that there's a war between men and women, a fight to the death," he once said, perhaps only slightly tongue-in-cheek: "That is, a fight to the psychic death, a struggle for supremacy and a ruthless and vicious contest of wills."[10] His lyrics (although not his collaborations) required women to be essentially separate from men – most of his work mourns, celebrates, or puzzles over the difference.[11]

Yet Leonard's masculinity is so wrapped in his feelings about the sacred, and his relationships with women, that in his poetry we often cannot tell if he is chasing women, God, or himself. With typical self-awareness he jokes about this ambiguity: "Come down to my room / I was thinking about you / and I made a pass at myself."[12] Or another example:

but all I ever see
is you or You
or you in You
or You in you

Confusing to everyone else
but to me
total employment[13]

Near the end of her biography, Simmons calls Leonard "a poet who
... seemed to be born to be a soldier or a monk."[14] Such metaphors
tell us much about Leonard's masculinity. In his youth, boys were
raised with toy guns, and sometimes real ones. I know this from personal experience – growing up in western Canada only two decades
later, I received my first rifle at age sixteen, and was expected to hunt
with it on the family farm. Sometimes my breakfast depended on
my success.

Leonard's earliest memories focus on "the beauty of our weapons"[15]
– taking down his father's wartime pistol and holding it in his hands.
Simmons writes that Leonard's childhood dream was to "fight wars
and win medals – like his father had done, before he became this in-
valid who sometimes found it hard to even walk up stairs ... nursed by
Leonard's mother."[16] Many of Leonard's poems, "The Traitor,"[17] "The
Warrior Boats,"[18] "Field Commander Cohen,"[19] and "Ballad,"[20] among
others, echo the fantasies of a young boy growing up in North America
in the postwar years. Leonard may have been absent a father, but he had
a soldier's exploits as shadows of his father's company. In his twenties,
the figure of the "brave partisan," a Hemingway-like freedom-fighter
artist, also appears. Cohen's deep friendship with the older poet Irving
Layton may not be unrelated to this valorization of Hemingway.

Paul also lived in a military society. He used similar military
imagery.[21] He sometimes refers to his male associates as "fellow
soldiers" for Christ.[22] Elsewhere he compares himself to a soldier

for his right to receive pay for his work of spreading the message about Jesus.[23] Military allusions form a backdrop especially to his letter to the Christ-followers at Philippi. Such images were natural for Paul, who spent his life in Roman cities where militarized police were a common sight. But the images were also useful for Paul in his descriptions of his discipline and self-reliance, which he linked to an attitude of stoicism.[24]

Self-sacrifice and discipline are hardly exclusively male values. But they are identified with a certain brand of masculinity that Paul and Leonard share very strongly with each other across the millennia:

> I have learned to be content with whatever I have.
> I know what it is to have little, and I know what it is to have
>   plenty.
> In any and all circumstances I have learned the secret of being
>   well-fed
> And of going hungry,
> Of having plenty and of being in need.[25]

In both the ancient and the modern world an important criterion of masculinity has been a man's physical appearance. The only description we have of Paul, found in the second-century *Acts of Paul and Thecla*, is somewhat contradictory. But what it does say of the apostle's physical appearance – bowed legs, short, balding, a monobrow – is less than complimentary by usual societal standards, whether ancient or modern. Remarkably, despite his careful sartorial stylings, a National Film board of Canada 1965 documentary provides ample proof that even when young, Leonard had an "old man's stoop." At one point in the documentary, he gets up from a hair stylist's chair and asks her: "Can you do anything about my body?"[26]

In a passage strongly reminiscent of our evidence of Paul, Leonard's final years are described as a time when he had "come to love this life of the road, the small closed community of supportive fellow travellers, the almost military regime."[27] But where Leonard (and Jesus, and Peter, and many of the earliest Christ missionaries mentioned in Paul's letters) travelled in mixed gender groups, often in male-female pairs,[28] Paul seemed for the most part to travel either alone or with Timothy or Sosthenes, whom he mentions as co-senders of his letters. Likewise, despite Leonard's actual collaborations with Sharon Robinson, Anjani Thomas, Rebecca De Mornay, and Jennifer Warnes, his work celebrates aloneness and aloofness, especially from women.[29]

Both depended at times upon financial sponsorship from women and engaged with women as coworkers. Yet both maintained a distance from women – Paul's distancing from women was quite literal in his celibacy, and Leonard's was at least performed in his writing but also evident in his problems with commitment and his often-expressed fear of being pinned down to one romantic partner. In the end, there is a calculated solitariness to the self-presentations of both men. Notice the physical hierarchy expressed in Leonard's lyrics, a topography that mirrors a gendered hierarchy of assumed artistic merit:

> I know you really loved me
> but, you see, my hands were tied.
> I know it must have hurt you
> it must have hurt your pride
> to stand beneath my window
> with your bugle and your drum
> while I was waiting
> for the miracle to come.[30]

In many of Leonard's poems, women are portrayed as conquests, a metaphor that inevitably casts them in some way as men's enemy.[31] In the gender war there are winners and losers, truces and treaties and stalemates, and there may well be an occupation and a resistance.

The poem just quoted was part of Leonard's proposal of marriage to Rebecca De Mornay. Note how even there he expresses his reaching out to her as capitulation.[32]

When the poet and the husband cannot be the same person, committed love can hardly be anything other than capitulation. "There are no traitors among women," Leonard writes, "Even the mother does not tell the son / they do not wish us well."[33] The conflict is *not* between the erotic and the spiritual, which inevitably fuse for Leonard. It is between domestic bliss and a troubled but ultimately more productive and blessed – and seemingly for Leonard, exclusively male – longing for the transcendent. Here Leonard was sadly typical of male artists employing what Myra Bloom (quoting Martin Jay) calls the "aesthetic alibi" that art justifies loutish behaviour.[34] Note how this portrayal of the gender relationship on the part of the male artist also acts to relegate the female to the non-transcendent, or bodily. The association of women and bodily preoccupations (as opposed to spiritual or intellectual concerns) is a consistent theme in Leonard's lyrics. It was a slur against women in a few early Jewish writers like Ben Sirach and Philo which took deep hold in early Christianity, found for example in ancient treatments of Eve.[35]

Fans of both Leonard and Paul have wondered whether each of these men helped create a new and more egalitarian type of masculinity. Sadly, in both cases, the answer seems to be no. Their *reception* may have sometimes helped to push masculinity in new directions. But that is different from saying these two men themselves were on such a quest. It's true that Paul wrote this:

I am content with weaknesses, insults, hardships, persecutions, and calamities for the sake of Christ;
For whenever I am weak, then I am strong.[36]

Unfortunately, however, talking about weakness does not signify that Paul was envisioning a new kind of masculinity that moved beyond the power dynamics of Roman society. Instead, he was attempting to turn his misfortune into an advantage. He was stating that his physical trials made him more of a Roman male, not less. This was also how he turned the emasculating image of Christ crucified into a more manly, stoic Christ, in the first chapters of 1 Corinthians.[37] Paul compared himself to the triumphant figure on the cross: "I am even more manly than most Roman men," he insists, "because, like the Christ I portray, I am able to endure sufferings stoically, and for the sake of others." Military and athletic imagery helped Paul make this point.[38]

Similarly, while over the years Leonard's poetry evolved from poet-soldier to poet-lover and finally to poet-mystic, the gendered imbalance of power is rarely given up. Leonard portrayed himself as vulnerable and easily wounded. But such admissions were strategic. He attached his reputation to the allegedly higher moral (but not artistic) principles represented by women rather more than women themselves, as real persons with their own agency. Of his long-time partner Marianne, Leonard once said: "It wasn't just that she was the Muse, shining in front of the poet. She understood that it was a good idea to get me to my desk."[39]

Lebold describes Leonard as a classic troubadour, whose obsession with women alternates between love and fear.[40] The female body is portrayed in such work as a shrine where one may worship the divine. Leonard even wrote, more than once, about the female body transforming into light.[41] Of course Leonard loved women, to the extent he allowed himself. But like some other artists, one wonders if it was real people he loved, or what those real women could inspire in him. There was no art without the muse. As his words about Marianne show, Leonard could not, or would not, prioritize the muse over the art.[42] As feminist as such an artist may attempt to be, the dynamics remain, in the most important ways, misogynist.

There is something abstract, almost gnostic, in Leonard's intentionally ambiguous appraisals of his female muses. According to him, the male poet has to be careful: if he lingers too long, the woman's body may turn into a place of the (male) soul's entrapment in mere matters of the world (read: domestic drudgery). "I would say that marriage today is a much more difficult, gruelling, and severe discipline than any monastic order could impose on its members," he once said. "Marriage today is the monastery."[43] Sadly but resolutely, and for the sake of a divine mission, the male poet must therefore turn his back on "the precious ones [he] overthrew / for an education in the world."[44]

When it came to defining what kind of relationship he shared with any particular woman, Simmons notes that Leonard's skills at deflection never flagged.[45] In "So Long, Marianne," Leonard wrote:

You know I love to live with you
but you make me forget so very much
I forget to pray for the angels
and then the angels forget to pray for us [46]

Remarkably for an ancient man, Paul's artistry is based on much more gender-neutral foundations. By contrast to Leonard, Paul is less interested in being the lover than the matchmaker between the people (of any gender) as bride, and Christ as groom. Nonetheless, his metaphors betray a decidedly male-centred cast.[47] To the followers in Corinth, he wrote:

I wish you would bear with me in a little foolishness. Do bear
with me!
I feel a divine jealousy for you,
for I promised you in marriage to one husband,
to present you as a chaste virgin to Christ.[48]

The Corinthians are presented in Paul's letter as if they are wayward women who have gone astray after another unfaithful lover (perhaps someone like Leonard!). By employing this trope, he endorses the ancient myth of women as unstable and prone to wildness and men as self-possessed and steady, and therefore women's guarantors of safety. By Leonard's time, the definitions of "male" and "female" characteristics had changed somewhat. But the myth of such binaries persisted.

Neither man belonged to the highest echelons of society.[49] Certain indicators of their status – Paul's literacy and his free status, Leonard's family's credentials in the Jewish community – were indicative of higher ranking. Others, such as being Jewish in 1950s Montreal or a Jewish craftsman in the Roman Mediterranean, came with limits (Leonard's stardom overcame the outsider status of which his early poetry shows he was painfully aware). At least for a time, such status inconsistency made Leonard and Paul what Homi Bhabha identifies as "liminal" men[50] who assert themselves while living out conflicting levels of authority (and thus masculinity) at the same time.

In the end, neither Paul nor Leonard revolutionized masculinity. While neither fell completely into his society's categories of "normative masculinity," nonetheless both still performed their gender in ways expected of them. However, there is one place where both Leonard and Paul's masculinities might be seen to at least hint at new directions. There is a remarkable parallel between Leonard's words in "I'm Your Man," and Paul's in 1 Corinthians 9, about becoming all things to all people:

> For though I am free with respect to all,
> I have made myself a slave [that is, unmanly] to all,
> So that I might win more of them …
> To the weak I became weak,
> So that I might win the weak.
> I have become all things to all people,
> that I might by all means save some.[51]

Compare Paul's promises of his flexibility to Leonard's:

> If you want a lover
> I'll do anything you ask me to
> If you want another kind of love
> I'll wear a mask for you
> If you want a partner
> take my hand, or
> if you want to strike me
> down in anger
> here I stand
> I'm your man[52]

As elsewhere in their writing, Paul sounds defensive, and Leonard coy. However, both men at least *point* to a flexibility and toward new ways of relating to others, including women. Whether or not they personally managed to break free of the expectations of their respective societies – or even wanted to – their words helped shape successive generations of readers and listeners to imagine new ways of performing masculinity.

TEXT MEDITATION

Listen to: "I'm Your Man," *I'm Your Man* (1988).

Compare the portrayals of masculinity in the following:

> My friends are gone and my hair is grey.
> I ache in the places where I used to play.
> And I'm crazy for love but I'm not coming on.
> I'm just paying my rent every day in the tower of song.
> (Cohen, "Tower of Song," *Stranger Music*, 363–4)

Yet whatever gains I had, these I have come to regard as loss
    because of Christ.
More than that, I regard everything as loss
because of the surpassing value of knowing Jesus Christ my
    Lord. For his sake
I have suffered the loss of all things,
And I regard them as rubbish,
in order that I may gain Christ and be found in him
    (Philippians 3:7–9a)

FURTHER READING

Studying figures ancient and modern through the lens of gender is not just scholarship about gender, but simply good, complete, scholarship (there is a reason Simmons titled her biography *I'm Your Man*).

On Cohen's masculinity, again see Schneller, "Cohen's Tales of Seduction Look Different through a #MeToo Lens" as well as Bloom, "The Darker Side of Leonard Cohen."

For an excellent and brief introduction to how masculinity helps us understand Paul and the ancient world better, see Parks, Sheinfeld, and Warren, *Jewish and Christian Women in the Ancient Mediterranean*, especially the sidebar on "Toxic Masculinity" on pages 110–11.

For more on Paul's unusual use of "maternal" images in his letters see Emmett, "The Apostle Paul's Maternal Masculinity."

For a good discussion of how widely defined "normative masculinity" could be in the ancient world, and how studies of masculinity have influenced our understanding of figures like Paul, see Marchal, "Queer Studies and Critical Masculinity Studies", 261–80, especially pages 266–70.

7 Everybody Knows

Leonard and Paul's Beguiling Rhetoric

Every year I begin my *Introduction to Paul* course by reading the letter to Philemon with my students. Philemon is short. It takes less than ten minutes to go through – so long as I can keep from excitedly interrupting my class to point out the strategic rhetoric Paul is putting to such fine service. By the time we've finished analyzing Philemon's twenty-five verses, we have a whole new respect for how ancient speakers crafted arguments. Students inevitably tell me they've learned a few tricks of persuasion themselves.

We need to remember that *all* of Leonard and Paul's works are performances. This is easy enough to say about Leonard, a professional performer. However, since "performance" tends in our culture and time to imply something false or unreal, those who consider Paul a saint might be surprised, even offended, to hear such an observation. Yet there is no denying that both men carefully crafted what they wrote to evoke specific audience responses. Paul considered it his divinely ordained duty to manipulate his readers toward certain reactions.[1] I think Leonard did as well.

A powerful characteristic of Leonard's poems and lyrics is that they are dialogic. This means they are often written in the second person, addressed to a "you" with whom the listener or reader automatically identifies. Second-person immediacy is characteristic of prophetic speech. From "show me the place" to "coming back to you," Leonard's use of pronouns turns artistic communication into a conversation demanding a response. Paul's letters do the same.

We know Paul's letters were delivered orally, or performed, for one simple reason: they were addressed to groups of people *most of whom couldn't read*. The vast majority (85 to 95%) of the population of the Roman Empire in the first century were illiterate.[2] Among the few who were not, there were varying degrees of skill; some were trained to copy written text or deliver an oration but not to comprehend it, while only a tiny fraction could compose original material.[3] The idea of a private individual reading silently and alone would have been foreign to most, since it would have depended on a level of public education unknown in Paul's day. A good analogy for how Paul's letters were received by his contemporaries might be to think of a church or synagogue with a lector publicly performing a text. The lector would have been well trained in how to speak and how to comport themselves physically. They might have followed certain conventions, including modulations of pose and of voice, that might seem flamboyant to our modern ears.

Paul's letters would have been presented by a messenger such as Phoebe or Timothy, people mentioned in the letter as co-senders. When his letter to the Romans commends to them "our sister Phoebe, a deacon of the church at Cenchreae, so that you may welcome her," it was most likely Phoebe herself who brought the letter and delivered it aloud. Ancient teachers of rhetoric like Quintilian spill a lot of ink on how such messengers should stand, where they should look, how they should vary their pitch and inflection, what they should do with their hands, when they should pause, and even what they should wear. The role of the messenger was all-important for a verbal communication such as a letter from Paul. For instance, we can be certain that in Corinth, when Timothy spoke out Paul's words "Now, concerning the collection,"[4] Paul had coached him to look at one or more key persons in the assembly, those who would be crucial to the fund-raising.

Of course, while the web is full of videos of Leonard – from his final tour to sold-out global amphitheatres, to him ordering a cheese sandwich in 1965[5] – there are no recordings of Paul's or his messengers' live performances. Nonetheless we should remember that they were every bit as carefully orchestrated and performative as Leonard's concerts.

If we overlook the design Paul and Leonard built into their writings, it means we are being manipulated without realizing it, making us even more susceptible to their persuasions. Whether it is Paul's rhetoric or Leonard's personification, "everybody knows" that the best sales gimmick is one the customer never sees.

> Everybody knows that the dice are loaded. Everybody
> rolls with their fingers crossed. Everybody knows the
> war is over. Everybody knows the good guys lost. Everybody knows the fight was fixed: the poor stay poor, the
> rich get rich. That's how it goes. Everybody knows.[6]

Both Paul and Leonard use intentional and structured persuasion. Consider the example just given. Leonard keeps repeating "Everybody Knows" at the beginning of each line of his piece. If it were an ancient audience, listeners might have been confused by the pop music (in Leonard's 2009 tour), or the jazz guitar and gospel harmonies that backed up the same song in 2013. But they would have recognized *exactly* what he was doing when he repeated the first line of the song again and again.[7] The repetition of a phrase at the beginning of every verse was, and is, called *anaphora*. It was taught in ancient elementary-school rhetoric. It's a particularly effective way of solidifying a message. Think of Martin Luther King Jr's continuous repetition of "I have a dream," which worked so well that we now call his famous 1963 speech by that name.

Leonard and Paul also shared other common rhetorical strategies. *Prosopopoeia* (pronounced proh-zoh-pop-ee'-ah) is the technique of creating an imaginary speaker, so as to engage in a mock debate. Notice Leonard's use of *prosopopoeia* in the following:

You say I took the Name in vain;
I don't even know the name.
But if I did, well, really, what's it to you?[8]

My point is that no one individual necessarily accused Leonard of not knowing "the Name." Rather, setting up the song this way with an imagined interlocutor helped Leonard write it. Much of his verse is in the second person, written to an imaginary, or sometimes a thinly disguised,[9] "you." Nor is the "you" always an opponent: it might be Leonard's lover, his confidante, his God, or even some part of himself. The poetry works best when Leonard leaves us unsure:[10]

You got me singing
Even tho' the news is bad
You got me singing
The only song I ever had[11]

Paul also employs *prosopopoeia*. The technique still confuses historians trying to reconstruct the Pauline assemblies in Galatia, Corinth, and elsewhere. Too often we assume there was a real individual or group behind one of Paul's scathing comments.[12] For instance, when Paul says "Is the law then opposed to the promises of God? Certainly not!"[13] it doesn't mean the Galatian assemblies themselves necessarily thought this. The question is rhetorical. He is building an argument. Like the advertisement that barks, "You say: 'I could never afford this kitchen device'... but you can!" the truth may be that Paul set up opponents in *theory* to press home an important point *in fact*. The opening lines of 1 Corinthians are a particularly vexing example:

For it has been reported to me by Chloe's people[14]
that there are quarrels among you,
my brothers and sisters. What I mean is that each of you says,

"I belong to Paul," or I belong to Apollos,"
or "I belong to Cephas," or "I belong to Christ."[15]

Much ink has been spilled trying to reconstruct the so-called par-
ties of Corinth according to these affiliations. But the fact that Paul
includes a group that says, "I belong to Christ" seems designed to
make the others look ridiculous. What follower in Corinth *would not*
want to say they were part of the Christ group? Paul's purpose is to
counter what was likely a very real divisiveness on the part of the
Corinthians, not necessarily to list a number of actual groups. He
may even have been inventing names in order to show how ridiculous
such divisiveness was.

This is not to say real situations are not behind Paul's (or
Leonard's) words. But the art with which both Leonard and Paul
wrote means we should be wary of sketching the audience (or even
the artist) too closely from their work. Exaggeration, flattery, ridi-
cule, and invention are all tools in the hands of a good orator. Both
caricatured themselves as well as others. As Gager points out, "If you
miss Paul's rhetorical strategies, you will get him wrong."[16]

Where Leonard is allusive, however, Paul commands. Where Paul
is usually direct, Leonard is typically coy. There are many uncertain-
ties about what Paul might have meant in a given passage, but most
exist because we simply cannot retrieve the original historical context. By contrast, Leonard made his career out of *intentional* artistic
ambiguity. As Mus points out: the "power of the artistic language in
Leonard Cohen's work lies mainly in suggestion."[17] His lyrics are so
powerful, and so many people relate to them, precisely because their
ambiguity creates a container into which the listener pours their *own*
experience of themselves, of their love, or of the divine.

In my classes I show how Paul used three tested and true techniques
of ancient rhetoric. The ancients called them *ethos*, *pathos*, and *logos*.
Leonard, who was once the president of McGill's university debating

society and who had imbibed so much of scripture and religious
tradition by heart, knew these techniques well. *Ethos* is an argument
that works by appeal to someone's character, *pathos*, by appeal to the
emotions, and *logos*, by appeal to a structured argument. For example:

I will be terribly despondent if you finish the book and don't
remember at least one of these three rhetorical techniques. Notice
what I'm doing? *Pathos*. I am appealing to your emotions, your possible
empathy or guilt, by mentioning my sadness, in order to obtain a desired
result: that you remember *ethos*, *pathos*, and *logos*. I am persuading
you to remember using an emotional tactic.[18] Seesengood notes
that "Paul is emotional. His letters ... drip with pathos, anger, and
emotional manipulation."[19]

Now look at the opening words of Philemon:

When I remember you in my prayers, I always thank my God
because I hear of your love for all the saints and your faith
    toward the Lord Jesus.
I pray that the sharing of your faith may become effective
when you perceive all the good we may do for Christ.[20]

Paul's language is confusing. Is he really complimenting Philemon?
If so, why does he immediately go on to make it sound as if Philemon
actually has more to do *before* he should be complimented?[21] The text
makes more sense if we think of it in the same way we might an em-
ployer who goes on and on in a meeting about how important our
team spirit is (building up our reputation), only to then announce she
is looking for a volunteer.

"Buttering someone up" is an ancient art that requires knowing oneself and one's needs, and being able to read others. The ancients called
this section of a letter the *exordium*. The *exordium* works because it appeals
to our character, using the technique of *ethos*: "Everyone knows you're
the most generous person in the family – now, may I have your cake?"

Wasn't hard to love you
Didn't have to try
My Oh My Oh My[22]

Ethos arguments are ego arguments – they rely on the fact that we will want to be seen by others in certain ways. *Ethos* arguments can be aimed at convincing us we are lovable, as in Leonard's example, but they are also used to sell anything from beer to war. Far more effective than information about a product is an argument that convinces us we're the *kind* of person who would naturally, without thought, buy that product or participate in that cause. Leonard was a master of *ethos*. *Ethos* arguments lean in, using intimacy to convince us we are a *type* of person. That we belong in a certain kind of club. That we should act in a certain way:

Confident of your obedience,
I am writing to you
Knowing that you will do
even more than I say.[23]

That was Paul. He used every tool in the book to convince Philemon to excuse the enslaved Onesimus. One of the remarkable aspects of the letter to Philemon is that even while seeming supportive of Onesimus, it actually reinforces the fact of his powerlessness. Onesimus (the name means "useful") is the subject of the discussion but is never himself allowed a voice. Much in the same way as many male authors "think with" women,[24] here Paul is thinking with the enslaved body of Onesimus. He is playing a high-stakes rhetorical game with Philemon over the fate of a person who is never given a voice in the letter.[25] During the long, long history of people from abolitionists to slave-owners reading this letter to prove their points, Onesimus himself usually continued to be denied a say.

Although the historical situation behind the letter to Philemon is somewhat cloudy, the outcome Paul wanted was Onesimus's pardon. The only person who could do that was Philemon. So Paul used *ethos* to describe to Philemon the *kind* of individual who would excuse an enslaved person, and then let Philemon live up to Paul's *ethos*.

Leonard often pulls off this rhetorical ploy. In his hands, it's more of an enjoyable hustle (the undercurrent of many a successful hustle being the whiff of intimacy). "Everybody knows" makes us feel we're elbow to elbow with the singer under a bare light bulb, sharing a whiskey, hearing his most unguarded thoughts. To my mind, this is where Leonard excels. He is the poet of the quiet midnight conversation, the dark revelation, everyone's ally or lover who assures us that, faults and all, we're known. Whether we are the lover or the beloved, he makes us see ourselves in his words. Leonard somehow manages to do all this while still casting himself as naïve and defenseless, the open-eyed and innocent partner we have to excuse for his magical gift of attention:

Dance me through the panic
till I'm gathered safely in
Lift me like an olive branch
and be my homeward dove
Dance me to the end of love[26]

To a gifted rhetorician, facts are not the most important aspect of an argument. What is important is the dance – the *experience* we live through their words. The way we know Paul is through his letters, and Leonard is through his poetry. Think of how Paul describes himself and other apostles to the Christ followers at Corinth:

To the present hour we are hungry and thirsty,
We are poorly clothed and beaten and homeless,
and we grow weary from the work of our own hands. [But]

When reviled we bless; when persecuted we endure;
When slandered, we speak kindly.[27]

Paul convinces his listeners by describing himself and inviting them
to identify with him. We should never forget the art in these words.
Both Leonard and Paul penned works they intended should stand in
for them. Leonard went so far as to propose marriage via song; he
let the lyrics do the asking.[28] Paul didn't need to travel physically to
Philemon to speak on behalf of the enslaved Onesimus: he let the
letter's performance do the convincing.

The term for such writing is "speech-act." Speech-acts are words that
do the thing being described (think: "I now pronounce you husband and
wife," "You're fired," "I apologize," or, "Let there be light"). Speech-
acts not only convey information; the words themselves change something. The same can be true of music, or poetry, or revelatory speech.
Christopher Partridge notes that "a piece of music becomes an event
that acts on a person, does something to a listener, stimulating the creation of an affective space within which meaning occurs."[29] So Leonard:

I heard of a man
who says words so beautifully
that if he only speaks their name
women give themselves to him.[30]

Or Paul, in the same way but to a very different purpose:

Though I am bold enough in Christ to command you to do
    your duty,
yet I would rather appeal to you on the basis of love – and I, Paul
do this as an old man, and now also as a prisoner.[31]

Biographical details for Paul are slim, while Leonard was famous
for refusing to specify exactly what his lyrics might mean. He was

well aware that his fans created meaning from his intentionally ambiguous verse. Paul's ambiguities were more accidental, and had far more painful consequences, from violence against women to systemic anti-Semitism. Given the persuasiveness of their words, they should be studied as much through their audiences' responses – that is, through what people have *wanted* to hear – as through what they themselves actually said.

In the end, we have to ask how much of what we think we know about these two comes only from our reactions to their carefully crafted self-presentations, their performances of self. Who was Leonard beneath his monkish robes and rakish suits? Who was Paul behind his statement that "it is no longer I who live, but Christ who lives in me"?[32]

Both writers used the tools of rhetoric to create and reinforce a story (many might say a myth) about themselves. They may have fervently believed those stories, since we all believe the myths we create about ourselves. Additionally, these self-presentations may have become more and more true over time. But what we believe we know about Leonard and Paul because of their stories may not be the entire truth about them. Leonard didn't break into success as early or as widely as he wished. When his relationships with women ended, it was rarely as reasonably and gently as his poetry implies. Paul may have repeatedly called himself an apostle. But many others in the early Jesus movement did not want to give this title to someone who had joined the movement much later than they had, and had not actually been one of Jesus's contemporary followers. Even the book of Acts, which tries valiantly to smooth over first-century tensions, barely uses the title when referring to him. When Paul does backpedal on his claim to apostleship, however, it is only to double down:

> For I am the least of the apostles, unfit to be called an apostle,
> because I persecuted the church of God.
> But by the grace of God I am what I am,
> and his grace toward me has not been in vain.

On the contrary, I worked harder than any of them.[33]
Compare Paul's self-deprecation, that turns into boasting, to Leonard's sly self-compliment:

> I was second to none
> but I was never best
> I was old and broke
> so I could not rest[34]

Another rhetorical device Leonard and Paul shared was to employ
self-deprecation proactively. They forestalled or moderated criticism
by being the first to mention their faults. By doing so, they were able
to define those faults, and turn them to their persuasive purposes. For
instance, Paul writes to Corinth:

> When I came to you, brothers and sisters,
> I did not come proclaiming the mystery of God to you in lofty
> words or wisdom.[35]

Paul goes on to tell his hearers how the apparent weakness and foolishness of his message simply underline God's strength and the alternative wisdom of the gospel. Near the end of 2 Corinthians, Paul
repeats what he presents as a criticism of himself by others:

> For they say: 'His letters are weighty and strong,
> But his bodily presence is weak,
> And his speech contemptible.'[36]

What begins as self-criticism then turns into a veiled (or not so veiled)
critique of the other: "[but] let the one who boasts, boast in the Lord."[37]
    In a parallel way, Leonard is not above starting with self-criticism
only to use it to critique others: "You want to get there soon / I want
to get there last."[38] As for his behaviour, like Paul ("Did I commit a sin

by humbling myself so that you might be exalted?"),[39] Leonard lets us think that he simply couldn't help himself: "I had to go crazy to love you / You who were never the one."[40]

The consummately ambiguous artist, Leonard rhetorically employed the religious dynamic of confession and forgiveness so important to both Judaism and Christianity to describe either a reluctant lover or a reluctant penitent, or (typically) both.[41] He made pure poetry of the gap between words and actions. For Leonard, the word may even stand in for the action: "And all I've said was just instead, / Of coming back to you."[42]

Ultimately, Paul's letters and Leonard's poetry are powerful because their words do more just represent them. At least in their popular receptions, their best words *improve* upon the human beings who wrote them, and transcend the individuals' failings. Here Paul and Leonard join many others whose words lived on: Dorothy Day, Martin Luther King Jr, Jack Layton, Mistahimaskwa (Big Bear). Whatever personal faults some of these individuals may have had, their speeches still inspire us to move beyond ourselves.

Leonard was a master of persuasive speech. So was Paul. Both created not just their public images but whole worlds of transcendent longing, forgiveness, and hope that they invited us to inhabit together with them. "Have this mind among yourselves," says Paul, encouraging his followers to express their love through unity.[43] Leonard's poetry did the same, inviting listeners into an act of redemption tied to the proper reception of the poet's words: "If I didn't have your love / To make it real." [44]

TEXT MEDITATION

Listen to: "Everybody Knows," *I'm Your Man* (1988).

Compare the rhetorical tactics used by Leonard and Paul in the following:

> It's a shame and it's a pity
> The way you treat me now
> I know you can't forgive me
> But forgive me anyhow
>
> The ending got so ugly
> Even heard you say
> You never ever loved me
> Oh but love me anyway
> ("Anyhow," *The Flame*, 114)

Confident of your obedience,
I am writing to you
Knowing that you will do
even more than I say.
(Philemon 21)

FURTHER READING

For more on Leonard's use of language, see Mus and Trehearne, *The Demons of Leonard Cohen*.

On the use of rhetoric in early Christian texts, including Paul's letters, see Olbricht and Sumney, *Paul and Pathos*. For rhetoric in Pauline literature specifically, see Porter, "Ancient Literate Culture and Popular Rhetorical Knowledge," as well as Schellenberg, *Rethinking Paul's Rhetorical Education*.

8 Birds on a Wire

How Leonard and Paul Had No Choice

A fascinating similarity between Paul and Leonard is their sense of divine vocation. Paul's call seems obvious to millions of Christian faithful, from his pivotal vision to his end as a martyred saint and possibly the most famous missionary of all time. On the other hand, one could be forgiven for believing Leonard's glib observation that his career began when as a young man he realized the guy with the guitar got the girl.[1]

The truth is that for the greater part of Paul's life, his mission was not at all clear; it met with one obstacle after another and left many, per-haps most, of his contemporaries unconvinced or hostile. Conversely, and despite his disavowals, Leonard's poetry is packed full of his sense of ordination, whether at the hands of God, or Art personified (much the same thing, for him). His urge to speak was so strong that at one point he wrote that he needed to "tear the stitches from my throat."[2]

Both Paul and Leonard – Leonard more obliquely – saw them-selves as divinely appointed. Both wrote of a compulsion coming from above: neither could help themselves. They had no choice. They had to speak, to preach, to write, to sing. Paul describes his call in words borrowed from ancient prophets like Jeremiah and Isaiah:

> But when God, who had set me apart before I was born
> and called me through his grace, was pleased to reveal his Son
> > to me
> so that I might reveal him to the Gentiles,
> I did not confer with any human being[3]

Paul often identified himself as being enslaved by his call to God, even though a free and at least somewhat privileged ancient man calling himself a slave when surrounded by so many truly enslaved people seems problematic to us now. Seesengood notes that "Paul's central metaphor for Christian life and faith is slavery and servitude."[4] In a Roman world whose economy ran on forced labour and where a significant percentage of the population was enslaved, Paul had daily examples of the physical, sexual, and other forms of abuse inflicted on humans considered to be property. A significant number of those who followed him were likely the (real) enslaved.

Leonard too uses the metaphor of slavery. Often it is treated with a somewhat light-hearted beginning:

Like a bird on the wire
Like a drunk in a midnight choir
I have tried in my way to be free[5]

But the theme usually becomes darker, as in later lines of "Bird on the Wire," or in the words of "Show Me the Place," a piece which references Jacob at the well, in addition to having a strong Good Friday allusion. In many of his lyrics Leonard plays with a biblical trope, going back at least to Jeremiah,[6] that the compulsion to carry a message "from beyond" is inevitably also a curse. Prophets *must* be miserable. As a youthful poet, Leonard also linked his vocation to a romantic notion of the artist as unhappy and inevitably alone. While he tended to express such concepts ironically, suffering on behalf of others was for him not just artistic, but theological.[7] Jackson writes that Leonard's "combination of sublime lyrics, soulful music, and trenchant social commentary makes him [...] prophetic. A prophet embodies revelation and critique rather than concealment and comfort. Cohen has received many prestigious awards – even in his own country – but in the end, he's a spiritual witness rather than a popular hero."[8] Freedman nuances this view by describing him as less prophet than *cohen*: one who leaves a blessing, even if through his own suffering.[9] In light of Freedman's comment, it's interesting that the young Leonard makes the artist (that is, himself) a Christ figure, and the life of the artist a vicarious sacrifice:

Will minstrels learn songs
From a tongue which is torn
And sick be made whole
Through rents in my skin?[10]

Paul seems to have been of the same mind: solitude and suffering are the lot not only of the enslaved but also of the prophet, since the prophet has been captured by and made subservient to the divine message.[11] In some places, Paul describes himself as a specific type of enslaved male: a gladiator forced to confront superior opponents and facing death with nobility and honour.[12] The overall message from both writers seems to be that those whom God calls pay a heavy cost for that honour. Using poetic imagery of sacrificial rites unfamiliar to most of us, but which would have made sense to his Roman audience, Paul tells followers in the city of Philippi that

Even if I am being poured out as a libation
over the sacrifice and the offering of your faith
I am glad and rejoice with all of you[13]

A libation is wine, honey, or another drink poured over an offering or an altar prior to a sacrifice to the gods. Libations may also be poured directly on to the earth as their own offering. Paul says that he himself is the one being poured out – being emptied – for the sake of "his" people. The metaphor does not stop there. It is not enough for the apostle (or the divinely enslaved prophet) to suffer. If he is to be part of blessing others, and if it will cost him so dearly, he expects a response. The audience must join in, for the sake of the world:

And in the same way,
you must also be glad
and rejoice with me.[14]

Leonard's sense of purpose also solidified over the years. Early
on, he criticized fellow Montreal poet A.M. Klein for being a "priest"
when a prophet was needed.[15] While the prophetic mantle was not
one he explicitly claimed, his idea that he occupied the liminal position of a religious seer intensified as he embraced more strongly
his place within Judaism. Already in 1967, he said that "for want of a
better word [my role] is that of cantor – a priest of a catacomb religion
that is underground, just beginning."[16] In the song "Amen," Leonard
links suffering, vocation, and his own willingness to continue as a
spokesperson for the divine. Nicolet-Anderson writes that in this song
Cohen not only takes on this task explicitly, but that he goes further,
saying that the idea of seeking divine intervention needs reversing,
and that "it might be human beings who are better suited in their
brokenness to heal the divine."[17] With typical ambiguity, in "Amen"
Leonard may be talking about the divine, his vocation, or a lover. For
Leonard, the three were always somewhat interchangeable:

Tell me again
When I'm clean and I'm sober
Tell me again
When I've seen through the horror
Tell me again
Tell me over and over
Tell me that you need me then
Amen[18]

Leonard, being Leonard, was rhetorically reticent where Paul was
bold. Publicly, Leonard turned any straightforward talk of a divine
commission into double-entendres. He utters "Hallelujah" only while

tied to the kitchen chair.[19] When he writes that he came so far for beauty or that he left so much behind, it could as easily refer to a woman as to God.[20] Pamela Erens notes that the "sublime in Cohen is never very far from laughter."[21] But even when he is making fun of his monotone, gravelly voice, he frames the joke within a reference to divine compulsion:

> I was born like this, I had no choice
> I was born with the gift of a golden voice,
> and twenty-seven angels from the great beyond,
> they tied me to this table right here, in the tower of song.[22]

Paul might not share Leonard's sense of humour. But he shares the latter's awareness of compulsion, down to a heavenly summons:

> If I proclaim the gospel,
> this gives me no ground for boasting
> for an obligation is laid on me,
> and woe to me if I do not proclaim[23]

Later, to the same community, Paul inserts just a bit of his own mild humour while he waxes poetic about the costs of carrying the divine. This is one of the places in his letters where Paul's words and the way they're framed could almost be Cohen lyrics, built as they are on a series of paradoxes:

> We are treated as imposters, and yet are true;
> As unknown, and yet are well known;
> As dying – and see – we are alive;
> As punished, and yet not killed;
> As sorrowful, yet always rejoicing;
> As poor, yet making rich;
> As having nothing, and yet possessing everything.[24]

Near the end of their lives, both Paul and Leonard seemed reconciled to their fates. Their earlier struggles with their chosen paths have finally resulted in a kind of peace. In his own way, each could see how light shines through even the darkest times – and each still expected some darkness in his future. For Leonard, the medium helped get the message across, as he said when talking about his 1992 album *The Future*: "If I had just nailed that lyric to a church door like Martin Luther it would be a very grim manifesto. But it's attached to a very hot little track so the words dissolve into the music and the music dissolves into the words and I think you're left with pure oxygen."[25]

Just before embarking on his last voyage to Jerusalem, Paul wrote to the Jesus community in Rome that he was nervous about the flashpoints at the Jerusalem Temple but that he hoped soon to "come to you in joy and to be refreshed in your company."[26] It would be Paul's last letter, and his nervousness proved prophetic. Although the precise details are lost to history, his arrival in Jerusalem turned sour. It marked the beginning of the end for him and his project.

In his own final interview, Leonard spoke of prayer as the chance to remind God of responsibilities to humanity.[27] According to him, a prophet doesn't speak only on behalf of the divine, but also at times argues against God. From his earliest poems to his latest, he queries not only his own healing but the injustice and suffering inflicting the world. Leonard's last album, *You Want It Darker*, was released seventeen days before he died. For the title track he was backed up by the cantor and choir of Montreal's Congregation Shaar Hashomayim. Notice how similar Leonard's words are to Paul's, as he speaks of the divine compulsion:

Magnified and sanctified
Be Thy Holy Name
Vilified and crucified
In the human frame

Hineni Hineni
I'm ready, my Lord[28]

TEXT MEDITATION

Listen to: "Bird on a Wire," *Songs from a Room* (1969).

Compare:

> Paul, enslaved by Jesus Christ,
> called to be a messenger,
> set apart for the gospel of God[29]
>   (Romans 1:1)

"I've read the Bill of Human Rights
And some of it was true,
But there wasn't any burden left
So I'm laying one on you."[30]
    ("The Captain," *Stranger Music*, 342)

FURTHER READING

Mus and Trehearne, *The Demons of Leonard Cohen,* contains excellent commentary on the artistic compulsion behind Cohen's career.

On the use of slavery as a metaphor by Paul, see Glancy, "Slavery and the Rise of Christianity."

9 The Secret Chord

Leonard and Paul the Mystics

Most of us have only the vaguest idea what a mystic is. We imagine a fiery-eyed, half-naked prophet atop a pole. Perhaps we think of a nun or monk voluntarily shut into a room for thirty-five years or picture a guru meditating at the mouth of a cave atop a high mountain (not unlike Mount Baldy). Erens once enthusiastically described Leonard by saying: "For what is a saint but someone who needs to have nothing to touch, who pushes away human intimacy and comfort for a higher devotion?"[1] Following her lead, one might describe a mystic with phrases like: "communing with God," "living outside normal concerns and routines," or "marching to a different drum."

Mysticism is living life open to the possibility of direct experience of the divine. Mystics relish experiences the rest of us barely perceive, or perhaps even actively avoid. Mystics are plugged into different senses. They commune with the divine. They feel compelled. They hear angels:

I walked into this empty church – I had no place
    else to go – when the sweetest voice I ever heard
    came whispering to my soul. I don't need to be
    forgiven for loving you so much. It's written in the
    scriptures, it's written there in blood. I even heard
    the angels declare it from above … *there ain't no cure*
    … *for love.*[2]

Historically, those mystics who have tried to communicate their experiences have struggled to capture in precise words what they have gone through. Yet such moments are, by definition, *beyond* words. They are an experience of transcendence, beyond logic and language. Already in 1972 Leonard remarked: "Anybody who writes songs knows that it's nothing they command. You are the instrument of something else."[3]

Mysticism is ultimately about *unutterable* experience. This is exactly how Paul describes what happened to him:

It is necessary to boast; nothing is to be gained by it,
but I will go on to visions and revelations of the Lord.
I know a person in Christ who fourteen years ago
was caught up to the third heaven – whether in the body
or out of the body I do not know; God knows ...
caught up into Paradise and heard things that are not to be told,
that no mortal is permitted to repeat.[4]

Paul manages to humble-brag about his mystical experiences in the third person – without actually telling us what they were. He implies that he is under an obligation *not* to reveal what happened, and that his hearers should in any case never know.

In accounts of mystical experiences certain themes recur: communication with angels, heavenly travel (whether as a dream or not), otherworldly visions, and sometimes, divine ordination. Paul uses forceful language: he was "caught up;" he was seized by angels and taken to the heavenly world. He could not resist the journey, even if he had wanted to. To reiterate the theme of the last chapter, Paul was coerced (Leonard also uses the language of divine coercion, in songs such as "Born in Chains").[5] In 1 Thessalonians, our earliest surviving letter from him, Paul uses "caught up" language to describe what the apostle expects to happen to *all* Christ-followers very soon when the messiah returns:

Then we who are alive, who are left,
will be caught up in the clouds together with them
to meet the Lord in the air; and so
we will be with the Lord forever.[6]

As Freedman notes, Leonard had "an almost unique ability to draw on the best of every belief system he encountered, and as far as one can tell from his lyrics, he saw no conflict between any of them."[7] However, we need not look beyond Judaism for the source from which both Leonard and Paul draw their mystical outlooks. Casual Cohen fans might be tempted to focus on Leonard's time as a Zen monk. However, mysticism has an ancient and revered place within Judaism.[8] Isaiah's mouth is cleansed with a burning coal held by an angel.[9] Ezekiel is snatched up by the spirit of the LORD and dropped in a valley of dead bones and told to preach until the bones come to life.[10] Tobias is secretly accompanied by the angel Raphael disguised as his kinsman. The angel saves him with magic and the guts of a fish.[11] Abraham is taken up to the heavens in a chariot by the archangel Michael and is allowed to behold many secrets of the cosmos.[12] Drawing on these resources, the simple language used by Leonard in his song "You Have Loved Enough" seems to be about human love and regret but turns out to refer to a Jewish mystical tradition in which Rabbi Akiva and three other rabbis make a voyage to paradise.[13]

That term "voyage" is important. Since about the 1990s, those who study Paul have begun to understand Paul's description of his heavenly journey as an example of the *Merkebah*, or "chariot" mysticism relatively common in the period.[14] Carla Sulzbach notes that "in the Second Temple period and Late Antiquity, encompassing Rabbinic Judaism and early Christianity ... a virtual explosion in the production of [mystical] materials took place."[15] Paul's letters (and the experiences he writes about) show him at the extreme of the spectrum – the type of mystic who takes mystical visions quite literally.

For a mystic, what we think of as an apt metaphor may be a lived reality. For most people, "I was blinded by love the first time I saw you" is a cliché. In the mouth of a mystic, it may mean the person believes they can no longer see. The spiritual manifests in the physical. Mysticism turns intuition and feeling (things we find hard to describe) into visionary experience. It may be an experience as relatively common as being moved by a sunset or being in a long-term relationship "a thousand kisses deep."[16] Nicolet-Anderson notes that in Leonard's lyrics there is "a back and forth between sacred and profane that modifies both the notions of divine and human."[17] Paul likewise brings these two realms together constantly, in sometimes unusual ways.

For instance, Paul often uses the term "in Christ." Almost all contemporary Christians understand that term as an expression of a wish: something like "in solidarity," or "in hope." But for Paul it appears being "in Christ" was something much more like *possession*. The way he describes it, a person "in Christ" is absorbed into a solidarity with the resurrected Jesus, no longer "in him- or herself."[18]

We can illustrate how literally Paul took being "in Christ," from his advice to the Corinthian group. At one point he commands Jesus followers (again, he seems to only be talking to the males) not to frequent Corinthian brothels. Both within his own Judaism and within wider Greek culture, Paul could easily have used well-known moral teachings to argue against Christ-following men going to sex workers. But instead, Paul employs the unusual and mystical argument of being "in Christ." Sex makes two people one body, he says. Christ-followers must not be "one body" with a sex worker, whether free or enslaved,[19] in a brothel, and also one body with Christ. Otherwise, they force Christ to have sex with that person.[20] The logic seems bizarre – except to a mystic.

Leonard's collaborator Jennifer Warnes, whose tribute album helped lift his career out of the doldrums, noted that playing on tour with Leonard felt "like a religious experience, night after night."

She remarked that she and others felt "spiritually called" to work on
Famous Blue Raincoat.[21] Leonard's poetry certainly encouraged such
understandings, as did his personal practice: he drew his own face
constantly as a spiritual practice on ego and emptiness, but could not
resist the epithet: "It was the hat, after all."[22] He spoke of wanting
to leave behind his work, saying "I want my life to leave, to deposit
songs."[23] At the same time, he feared that the only image of him that
would be left would be the iconic suit.

Self-emptying looks to the divine as the container into which one
is emptied. Leonard's words of absorption, of union with the transcendent, are typical of mystics:

> You are my tongue, you are my eye,
>   My coming and my going.
>   O G-d, you let your sailor die
> So he could be the ocean.[24]

Compare this to Paul, whose words of prayer come from the transcendent as well:

> Likewise the Spirit helps us in our weakness;
> for we do not know how to pray as we ought,
> but that very Spirit intercedes with sighs too deep for words.[25]

"Too deep for words" is the mantra of the mystic. It would certainly work as the title of a Cohen poem! Yet despite the ineffability of
their spiritual experiences, neither Leonard nor Paul stopped trying
to communicate them. Pleshoyano describes Leonard's mysticism as
"poiesis," a creative act in which it is the intuition that "can grasp
something of the eternal through the temporal, something of the in-
finite through the finite."[26] However, each poet started at an opposite
end: Leonard with the human experience, Paul the divine revelation.
For both, there is a kind of melding of the physical world with the

spirit world, a "meaningful encounter of quotidian and sacred."²⁷ This
melding leads not only to communion with the divine, but also with
the community. Leonard alludes to this in one of the final poems he
included in *The Flame*:

> For I have been thru many lives
> & no one follows me
> I am what you were last night
> & I am what you'll be ²⁸

In a similar way, while dealing at a distance with a thorny problem of
church discipline Paul writes:

> For though absent in body, I am present in spirit;
> And as if present I have already pronounced judgement in the
>   name of the Lord Jesus
> On the man who has done such a thing. When you are assem-
>   bled,
> And my spirit is present with the power of the Lord Jesus,
> You are to hand this man over to Satan.²⁹

In these examples, Leonard and Paul claim more than just personal experience of the divine. They also claim to be *mediators* of
the divine, and to be able to lead others toward such moments.
Leonard invited listeners into the "furnace" where through art they
could be remade.³⁰ Both wrote that they were instruments through
which others could experience that-which-is-beyond-words. Leonard
sometimes wrote about himself in the third person (much like Paul
did about his mystical experience of the "third heaven"), and at other
times speaks in the divine first-person:

> He wants to write a love song
> An anthem of forgiving

A manual for living with defeat
A cry above the suffering
A sacrifice recovering
But that isn't what I need him to complete[31]

In 2009 Donald Grayston noted that Cohen had recovered a sense of holy "delight" and that he had "become in his eighth decade a spiritual teacher."[32] Leonard may have been surprised to have attained such stature, but Paul seems never to have doubted the office. He puts it like this, to the assembly in Corinth: "Think of us in this way, as servants [slaves] of Christ and stewards of God's mysteries."[33] Paul describes being chosen as a steward of divine mystery as a calling, but a dangerous, lonely, and heart-breaking one. Paul's language of being "poured out" for others is paralleled by Leonard's self-description when he says: "If thine is the glory, / Then mine must be the shame."[34] Elsewhere he hints at the danger of a prophetic calling:

It's coming for me darling
No matter where I go
Its duty is to harm me
My duty is to know[35]

The urgency evident in both Leonard and Paul's writings about their mystical experiences harkens back to themes not only of compulsion, but also of judgment. Paul warns in his oldest surviving letter of "the wrath that is coming."[36] In one of his few poems referencing his mother, Leonard's muse speaks as Micha but also as the divine presence that requires his voice. The poet ends with the cry:

I want to cross over, I want to go home,
But she says, "Go back, go back to the world."[37]

"Woe to me if I do not proclaim the gospel!" Paul wrote.[38] He also wrote the following:

> When I came to you, brothers and sisters,
> I did not come proclaiming the mystery of God to you
> in lofty words or wisdom …
> My speech and my proclamation were not with plausible
>   words of wisdom
> but with a demonstration of the Spirit and of power,
> so that your faith might rest not on human wisdom but
> on the power of God.

What were those "demonstrations of power" Paul describes? They were the traditional ways of proclaiming divine love that he, like Leonard, had inherited. The tradition was Jewish. For both Leonard and Paul, their ancient faith includes themes of covenant, the divine name, Torah, brokenness,[39] healing, community, and divine hope.

Ironically, comparing Paul and Leonard's mystical emphases means trying to put words to an experience that is by definition undefinable. Both Paul and Leonard sought to communicate their understanding of the mysteries of life, love, and death for a world that they were convinced needed to hear it. During Leonard's final tour, he would gather with his fellow musicians before going on stage to sing "pauper ego sum" (I am poor),[40] and would bless the crowd before leaving at final curtain call. As Freedman has pointed out, by doing this Leonard was living out his Judaism in a way that recognized his name: from time immemorial the *cohenim* have been responsible for giving blessings.[41] Paul similarly ended all his letters, including Romans, likely his last letter, with blessings.[42]

Faced with a transcendent power we cannot understand, we react with awe. Ultimately, mystics like Leonard and Paul react to the divine presence with communication, resistance, and submission. Paul ends one of his most heart-felt letters with the prayer:

Our Lord, come![43]

And Leonard with the words:

Hineni, Hineni
I'm ready, my Lord[44]

TEXT MEDITATION

Listen to: "Hallelujah," *Various Positions* (1984).

Compare the self-professed attitude of Leonard and Paul toward an encounter with the divine:

... even though
It all went wrong
I'll stand before the Lord of Song
With nothing on my tongue but Hallelujah
("Hallelujah," *Stranger Music*, 347)

Think of us this way, as servants of Christ and stewards of
    God's mysteries.
Moreover it is required of stewards that they be found trust-
    worthy.
But with me it is a very small thing that I should be judged by
    you or any human court ...
It is the Lord who judges me.
    (1 Corinthians 4:1–4)

FURTHER READING

For more on Cohen's mysticism see Freedman, *Leonard Cohen: The Mystical Roots of Genius*, especially chapter 4: "Heaven and Earth." On mysticism as a phenomenon of early Judaism and early Christianity, see Segal's article "Mysticism" in *The Eerdman's Dictionary of Early Judaism*.

10 Come Healing

Leonard and Paul as Witnesses to Brokenness and Redemption

By now one of the ironies of this book must be clear: Leonard was more "Christian" than Paul.

This is simply a fact of history. Of course, Leonard was not actually a *Christian*. He was a Jew – a point he had to insist on. The differences and similarities between Judaism and Christianity were a constant source of inspiration and (it seems) occasional vexation for Leonard. His first book of poetry, *Let Us Compare Mythologies*, frequently contrasts the bedrock faiths of his home city. In the final track of his album *Old Ideas*, he again contrasts the faiths explicitly – or at least, as explicitly as his lyrics ever allow. He talks about a "higher eye" where such differences are not consequential: "Though it all may be one in the higher eye / Down here where we live it is two."[1]

Always the diplomat, Leonard often spoke positively about Jesus, while avoiding comment on Christianity. When asked about the latter, he tended to bring the discussion back to Jesus: "in spite of what I know about the history of legal Christianity, the figure of the man [Jesus] has touched me."[2] Another time he said: "Outside of the organizational enterprise, which some applaud and some mistrust, stands the figure of Jesus, nailed to a human predicament, summoning the heart to comprehend its own suffering by dissolving itself in a radical confession of hospitality."[3]

Leonard's theological language here would not sound out of place in a Christian sermon. Such words illustrate that at the same time as he could stand outside it as a critic, Leonard was in a very real sense a descendant of Christianized European society. He was an inheritor of the long history of Christian culture. For better and worse, Leonard knew in his bones what Christianity *is*. Throughout his books and albums, he wrestled with Christian symbols, figures, language, and stories.

Paul never did any of this. It was impossible for Paul to do so. Christianity did not exist as a separate religion in Paul's lifetime – the gospels had not yet been written. All of the religion's contributions to art, literature, philosophy, and theology, as well as its dogmas, its persecutions, its triumphs, and its most abject failures – all of that lay in a future that happened after Paul.

Paul knew nothing of institutional or monumental Christianity. In fact, references throughout Paul's letters show he expected society as we know it to soon be over.[4] By contrast, Leonard lived two thousand years after Christ, and after Paul. His very first recorded lines of poetry show how Christian thought, art, and music helped shaped him, as it has so much of today's world.

Leonard speaks of "a cross on every hill." He writes, "Give me Christ or give me Hiroshima."[5] Christianity's influence on Leonard and his art goes much deeper than such examples, to the very way that he, and the rest of us in Western cultures, think about our world and ourselves. In his lyrics, Leonard returns again and again to the meaning of his life "against the fate that bends us down."[6] He was haunted by what Krister Stendahl called "the introspective conscience of the West."[7] Paul was not.

Leonard said a number of remarkable things in his "Acceptance Address for the Prince of Asturias Award" in 2011. Among them is the following:

> [Federico García Lorca] gave me permission to find a voice, to locate a voice;
> that is, to locate a self, a self that is not fixed, a self that struggles for its own existence.[8]

Leonard's references to a "voice," to a "self," and especially to having actually to *seek* a voice and a self – these are part of a cultural heritage shaped by millennia of Christian theology. "Who am I?" is a question that gained importance in the seventeenth century, after the work of the Christian philosopher René Descartes. Leonard felt that question in his bones, and it reverberates through his songs.

Like other ancients, Paul sometimes pondered the meaning of life. But he lived long before the modern preoccupation with individual authenticity.[9] As we see in some of the Psalms, what some have called the "turn to the self" (a questioning of what life means, from a personal standpoint) is not foreign to ancient Judaism. But it owes much more to the tortured ponderings of Augustine and the tradition Augustine left behind. Leonard sketched his own face regularly as a meditation on aging (and also as a Buddhist practice). Paul would have been mystified to watch him do it. Paul was an ancient. Leonard was a modern.

Leonard played at times with nihilism and its effects on identity:

Had to go crazy to love you
Had to let everything fall
Had to be people I hated
Had to be no one at all[10]

Joe Heschmeyer wrote about Leonard: "Ain't No Cure for Love," is at first glance a simple love song. The "surface to the song," as Cohen said, is the story of "a man who could not shake the feeling that he had lost the woman of his life and that there was no solution to this problem, and that even time was not a solution." Beneath the surface, however, was what Cohen described as a "kind of theological or philosophical position" – namely, that "the condition that most elevates us is the condition that most annihilates us, that somehow the destruction of the ego is involved with love," after which "you can never again feel at the centre of your own drama."[11] For Leonard, existential longing and divine connection are inseparably linked at the base of the human condition. They define us.

Paul would not necessarily have thought to answer the question: "Who are you?" by describing his *character*. Like any ancient person he answers with his lineage and his relationships. Paul says he is:

> circumcised on the eighth day,
> a member of the people of Israel,
> of the tribe of Benjamin,
> a Hebrew born of Hebrews.[12]

In other words, to the question "Who are you?" Paul answers: *These are my people.* This emphasis on relationship is not unlike the way many contemporary Indigenous writers continue to insist that human identity works: relationally.[13] This is also the way Paul wants his followers to define *their* new identities in Christ (many a biblical scholar points out that Paul would be surprised at the individualism of contemporary Western Christians). Whether from Philippi or Ephesus or Rome, the non-Jews to whom Paul preached were to understand themselves as adopted by baptism into the *family* of Abraham. That familial relationship was to define their new identity.[14] In very practical terms, Paul was advising that to change your community was to change your identity, and to change your identity would necessitate changing your community.[15]

This is not to say that Paul had *no* sense of his individual self, nor that Leonard lacked an awareness of community. Paul loved talking about his accomplishments. Having come late to the mission of apostle, he brags that he "worked harder than any of them."[16] While Leonard remained elusive to the end about the precise meaning of most of his songs, he was never shy about being part of the Jewish community. As the work "Born in Chains" implies, being "bound to a burden," was his communal birthright.

But much changes in two thousand years. Leonard and Paul inevitably show their time-period in reacting to the eternal question: Why is there such undeniable suffering in the world? To answer, Paul starts with the community. Leonard starts with the individual. Paul begins from the tragedy of a broken people, Leonard the tragedy of a broken life. Where Paul approaches individual relationships from the starting point of a divine encounter, Leonard touches on the divine by first focussing on the individual: often the sexual, erotic, individual. Each explores the psychology behind the human condition from their own society's starting point.

Like most of the rest of the contemporary world, Leonard grew up a child of what historians have called the Romantic period (or Romanticism), an early nineteenth-century movement in which many feel we are still living.[17] Romanticism focusses on the role of the individual, and from that vantage pays special attention to emotion, to nature, and to aesthetics in general (for an example, just listen to the lyrics of any popular song). Leonard's listeners, and Paul's contemporary audiences as well, are children of this Romantic shift in sensibility and self-perception. It points to why Leonard's phrases often seem so film-like, a quality we recognize and most of us instinctively appreciate:

Was it ever settled
Was it ever over
And is it still raining
Back in November[18]

One of the tropes (the recurring stereotypes) of Romanticism is that its heroes are tortured artists. From Lord Byron, after whom Leonard perhaps modelled himself as a younger poet, to Virginia Woolf, or more recently, the tragic and too-short lives of any number of other actors, singers, or painters, many of us find it only natural that a true poet or writer should somehow be a "tortured soul." Yet there is nothing that says the artistic life must necessarily be difficult. Leonard successfully transmuted his anxieties, his worries, and his grim reflections into song-writing gold, then did so a second time after being embezzled by his manager.[19] Living prior to the Romantic-era change in artistic sensibilities, the classical composer and organist Bach seemed to have had a fairly robust sense of self. In the same way, one of the profound realizations of recent biblical scholarship on Paul is just how untroubled the apostle's conscience seems to have been. A quote from one of his letters shows Paul completely without angst and self-doubt:

> If anyone has reason to be confident in the flesh, I have more:
> [I was …]
> as to the law, a Pharisee;
> as to zeal, a persecutor of the church;
> as to righteousness under the law, blameless.[20]

Note: Paul actually says he's "blameless"! In 2 Corinthians 5:10-11 Paul indicates he has no worries at all about appearing before the judgment seat of God, although he wonders about his listeners among the Corinthians. Of course, he sometimes writes as if he felt discouraged, even broken. But it may be an example of the *pathos* arguments discussed earlier. In 1 Corinthians, he writes:

> I came to you in weakness and in fear and in much trembling …[21]
> To the present hour we are hungry and thirsty,
> We are poorly clothed and beaten and homeless,
> And we grow weary from the work of our own hands.[22]

Paul says he knew what it is to suffer. But it is remarkable how little, in the midst of that suffering, he seems to doubt either the God who had called him, or his much-troubled mission to the non-Jews. About these he had an ongoing certainty that seems the opposite of

Leonard's public anxieties and depressions. Paul certainly did not live out any kind of modern conversion story. He was not a Christ-follower because of any dark night of the soul.[23] He *did* admit having once persecuted the movement, but apparently felt no guilt. Paul was utterly confident. He was a Christ-follower purely and simply because he had a vision. He believed the end-of-days resurrections had begun. He believed he had proof:

> But in fact Christ has been raised from the dead,
> the first fruits of those who have fallen asleep.[24]

Leonard, on the other hand, knew all about guilt. He was prone to self-blame, even if there was often some artifice to it, and even if in his final decades he showed a marked move toward self-acceptance. In the Prince Asturias Award speech already mentioned, Leonard states:

> As I grew older, I understood that instructions came with this voice.
> What were those instructions?
> The instructions were never to lament casually.[25]

A refusal to lament casually, *yet the insistence on lamenting,* marks the whole of Leonard's career. Laments form part of the Jewish scriptural tradition of Psalms and Prophets that both writers shared, studied, and learned. Mikal Gilmore, in the *Rolling Stone* obituary, called Leonard "the poet of brokenness."[26] Many of us love his words precisely because they give voice to our own brokennesses. Like the Psalms that some of Leonard's poetry resembles,[27] we hold his lines close in those moments when we know the profoundest losses, self-betrayals, guilt, regrets, and disappointments.

Both Leonard and Paul met the yawning emptiness of life by naming and embracing it. Leonard did it by way of the divine Name, Paul by pointing to the cross. Both ultimately felt that the Name – and the cross – commanded them to speak and sing in the emptiness and in some ways *against* that emptiness, even while allowing it to be creative. At one point in his letters, Paul wrote:

> To keep me from being too elated, a thorn was given me in
>   the flesh,
> a messenger of Satan to torment me …
> Three times I appealed to the Lord about this, that it would
>   leave me,
> but he said to me, "My grace is sufficient for you, for
> power is made perfect in weakness."[28]

This formulation of grace in weakness is transmuted by Leonard into the memorable image of light entering a cracked vessel. Nicolet-Anderson observes that "Cohen's songs illuminate the broken parts of human life, the frailties of human beings, and identify these fragilities as spaces where the sacred shines through."[29] In 1992, Leonard wrote his famously hopeful description of how we should act in light of suffering and brokenness:

> Ring the bells that still can ring.
> Forget your perfect offering.
> There is a crack in everything.
> That's how the light gets in[30]

"A Crack in Everything" means especially a crack in *human beings*. One of the deepest insights of both writers is that to be human is to be imperfect, in need of lifting up. In some ways, for each, the brokenness of humanity is precisely where divine agency and healing can occur. Honestly facing the brokenness is a precondition for healing.

Michael Posner writes that Leonard's "crack in everything" is grounded in Jewish mysticism. Posner says the line "actually derives from the Lurianic Kabbalah, from a premise known as the Shevirat HaKeilim, the breaking of the vessels. According to Luria [an early modern Jewish mystic], ten vessels originally contained the emanation of God's light. Too fragile to safely harbour it, they shattered, leaving the world in chaos. Only by a reunion of the male and female principles, a conceit deeply embedded in Cohen's work, can the vessels be repaired."[31] While Leonard (and Paul, in his way) were both interested in the "reunion of male and female principles,"[32] Posner misses that the concept goes back at least to classical Greece.[33] Importantly for our purposes, Paul also wrote a phrase reminiscent of Leonard's "crack in everything" a full two millennia before the singer. Paul metaphorically writes of divine treasure being carried in human containers:

> we have this treasure in clay jars,
> so that it might be made clear that this extraordinary power
> belongs to God and does not come from us.
> We are afflicted in every way, but not crushed;
> perplexed, but not driven to despair;
> persecuted, but not forsaken;
> struck down, but not destroyed.[34]

Paul's "clay jars," shattered Kabbalistic "vessels," and Leonard's "crack in everything" all exist within a long and rich tradition that has *always* found hope not despite, but *in*, human frailty. Whether it is the giant Goliath defeated by the small boy David (1 Samuel 17), or the armies of the tyrant Antiochus defeated by the rag-tag brothers (1 Maccabees), or by the widow, the children, and the elderly man (2 Maccabees), or the string of mighty military oppressors of Judaism defeated "by the hand of a woman" from Jael (Judges 4:17-23) to Judith (Judith 13:15), the historic victories of the ancient Israelites and the Hellenistic Judaism of Paul's day were *underdog* victories. There is no end of the weak and vulnerable as victors in ancient Jewish narratives. Both Leonard and Paul derived their appreciation for human broken-ness within this same Jewish tradition.

In his final years, Leonard became a pastoral figure for many of his fans, a sage for the world, what the New York Times called a "secular saint."[35] He appeared to move into a state of grace. It was a time when the longing quieted and his problematic obsessions with women ta-pered off, where he was not broken but "borderline."[36] In his final works there's an acceptance of ambiguity that he sets against his age, his cancer, and what he knew was his impending fate:

> I wonder what it was
> I wonder what it meant
> At first he touched on love
> But then he touched on death[37]

Given the perspective of Leonard's entire oeuvre, and of his last concerts, it might not be too much to add a concluding line: "And finally, he touched on hope." Despite a certain melancholy to many of Leonard's late lyrics, their elegiacal tone cannot hide hints of what the poet seems to believe is divine acceptance. It seems typical to me that the day before he died, in a text message to Rebecca De Mornay in response to a photo of her daughter Sophia De Mornay-O'Neil, he quoted Christian scripture (that is, the words of a first-century Jew): "Blessed are the peacemakers: for they shall be called the children of God."[38]

In Leonard's work one hears hints that even though in his early poetry he might have tried to claim a kind of messianic authority, it was at the end of his life that he felt more strongly in himself the commission he had so often imagined. Leonard's last writings and interviews seem to indicate that he saw his task not only as witness-ing to injustice and to the "light that gets in" but also actively healing humanity through his words – that is, taking on a priestly role in order to help "repair the broken world."[39] It's both an example of his Jewish identity, and of the deep implications of the Jewish festival of Shavu'ot, that he could put those hopes in words hearkening back to the ancestral longings of both his and Paul's people:

They're dancing in the streets – it's Jubilee
We sold ourselves for love but now we're free[40]

TEXT MEDITATION

Listen to: "Anthem," *The Future* (1992) and "Come Healing," *Old Ideas* (2012).

Compare the relationship with the divine pointed to by Leonard and Paul in the following:

And for this conversation
in the early morning light
I offer up these shabby days
that fray before your sight
Nor can I know how many more
will pass ere I'm unstrung
and all that's left this song you placed
upon your creature's tongue
     ("Every Pebble," *Stranger Music*, 400)

We do not live to ourselves, and we do not die to ourselves.
If we live, we live to the Lord, and if we die, we die to the Lord;
so then, whether we live or whether we die,
we are the Lord's.
     (Romans 14:7–8)

FURTHER READING

Leonard once wrote to his son, "I wanted to stand with those who clearly see G-d's holy broken world for what it is, and still find the courage or the heart to praise it."[41] At some point, perhaps, writing about light in darkness, or resurrection in death, one *becomes* what one does. The artist or writer begins to embody in themself the hope they portray. Robert Kory wrote about Leonard in the last months of his life that his "humility was genuine, and his gratitude unmistakable."[42] Simmons records the aged Leonard as saying, "we are all motivated by deep impulses and deep appetites to serve, even though we may not be able to locate that which we are willing to serve."[43]

For more reading related to this chapter, I point you again to Mus and Trehearne, *The Demons of Leonard Cohen*, and to Nicolet-Anderson, "Leonard Cohen's Use of the Bible: Transformations of the Sacred." Also of interest and related to this chapter is Gilmore, "Leonard Cohen: Remembering the Life and Legacy of the Poet of Brokenness" and Posner, "That's How the Light Gets In: Remembering Leonard Cohen."

To learn more about the "by the hand of a woman" trope in ancient Hebrew literature, see Parks, "Women and Gender in the Apocrypha," in *The Oxford Handbook of the Apocrypha*.

For an overview of a variety of approaches to the subject of Pauline studies known as "Paul's theology of suffering," see Davey, "Playing Christ: Participation and Suffering in the Letters of Paul," which offers a roadmap through recent scholarship on Paul's idea that believers must "participate" in Christ's suffering, and demonstrates how indispensable the experience of suffering is to Paul's concept of being "in Christ."

11 Thanks for the Dance

Leonard and Paul's Long Afterlives

If you were lucky enough to attend one of Leonard Cohen's last concerts, or if perhaps you've watched a video of one, you will have heard the opening speech he typically used. Returning to the spotlight after years of absence, Leonard would step on stage and say: "It's been fifteen years since I last toured. Back then I was 60 years old: just a kid with a crazy dream" (peals of laughter). "Since then, I've taken a lot of Prozac, Ritalin, Wellbutrin. I also studied religion and philosophy. They tried me on everything – but it was no use. *Joy kept breaking through*."[1]

Behind Leonard's reference to depression and his hopeful punchline sits a carefully constructed autobiographical narrative. Like many of us but more effectively than most, he crafted his image. He would have been happy with Leon Wieseltier's eulogy: "Leonard Cohen was the poet laureate of the lack, the psalmist of the privation, who made imperfection gorgeous."[2] As the saying goes, Wieseltier was on message.

The fact that Leonard carefully crafted his post-mortem image is *not* to argue that Wieseltier's eulogy is not true. Nor would I argue that Leonard didn't believe his own PR. However, in this final chapter, I would like to point out how Paul and Leonard's careful self-presentations ensured their works lived on after them, sometimes in surprising ways.[3]

Leonard's "wilderness time" – to use a biblical metaphor – happened in the 1980s. At that point his career had stalled, and he wondered if he'd have any heritage at all. As it turned out, the man in the suit succeeded despite his naysayers. From the '90s until his death, in his books and in opening monologues at his concerts, Leonard successfully enshrined his memory as a series of characters: the youthful troubadour of love, the middle-aged mystic and monk, the elder but still sexy statesman heroically fighting age and illness – and finally, the public priest whose music bestowed a benediction on the listener.

Leonard made sure his poetry supported the legacy by which he wanted to be remembered. His writing repeats his message of the endurance of longing, the beauty of a frailty embraced, and the possibility of redemption even in defeat.[4] Surprisingly, those three phrases – "endurance of longing, beauty of a frailty embraced, redemption in defeat" also map quite nicely on to Paul:

> We also boast in our sufferings, knowing that
> suffering produces endurance, and
> endurance produces character and
> character produces hope

Paul made the source of his hope clear: "God's love has been poured into our hearts through the Holy Spirit ... given to us."[5] Paul's language might seem far from the gritty lyrics of Leonard Cohen. But strip those words down two thousand years, and I suspect Leonard would admit he shared with Paul the experience of a terrible, liberating, life-absorbing sacred love, and the divine burden to share it with others. Freedman writes that Leonard's last album, *You Want It Darker*, is "an accusation, a rebuke to the power who deals the cards, heals the lame, radiates glory and, despite all this, condemns us to extinguish the flame."[6]

Ultimately, despite their strong input into the legacies they left behind, the memory of both figures will continue to be shaped by their constituencies. Their public images are built on what later readers have made of them, and how their words continue to be treasured and relied upon, especially in times of difficulty, love, and longing.

———

I started this book with my feet up on the Buddhist coffee table inherited from Leonard's house on Rue Vallières. Tenuous as that connection is, I rely on it to confirm my imagining that somehow I know him. In reality, like every other fan, time after time I have found and continue to find myself in the poet's lyrics. "Suzanne" makes me feel like more of a Montrealer. Leonard voices my regrets better than I ever could in "Famous Blue Raincoat." He holds longing to the light in "Coming Back to You." Times of heartbreak and sacrifice make me feel deeply known in "Show Me the Place." My secret moments of bitterness find expression in his "Everybody Knows."

You get the picture.

The power of good writing is that it draws us in and invites us to identify with it. Very good writing allows us to access feelings we barely realize we have. Both Leonard and Paul give words to such feelings. We take on the writers' sentiments and go through them, sometimes toward catharsis.

At the same time, it is instructive to remember ways in which most of us live at a great distance from Paul, and even from Leonard. We also learn a lot by *not* identifying quite so closely with these two poets of the human and the divine. Critical thinking always requires stepping back and looking at something from different angles. To that end, writing this book was a helpful exercise for me in meeting both writers' works "again for the first time."[7]

With Leonard, I needed to move past the falsely intimate (but oh so common) identification that made his songs the soundtrack of my life.[8] I needed to remember to see not just the beauty, but also the con, the hustle, and the misogyny. While identifying with the beauty of "Come Healing" it was good to remember the young Leonard in a bathtub writing "caveat emptor" on the bathroom tiles for the cameras of the National Film Board of Canada documentary crew. There, at the very beginning of his long career of image creation, he was self-consciously warning us: "Don't believe everything" you're about to see and hear.[9]

New Testament scholars since the Holocaust have worked to get to know Paul the apostle in *his* home, in the Jewish and Roman first century, not in our own world of post-Christendom individualism.[10] I encourage my students to hear in his message both its Hellenic rhetoric and its own first-century brand of urgent, apocalyptic Judaism. Stendahl states that it is important "to insist on a clear distinction between what a text meant according to its original intention, and what it came to mean and/or might mean at any later point."[11] Applied both to Paul's letters and to Leonard's song lyrics, this can be a liberating realization.

However, seeing these two on their terms, not ours, can also be bracing.

When I began, I thought perhaps my research into Leonard's life would diminish my admiration for him. That turned out to be the case for parts of his life, but not all of it. For instance, I am sure I'm not the only reader who shudders to read his biographer's description of Leonard's 1970s interview with writer and broadcaster Malka Marom: "Marom recalls, 'He was very whimsical. Soon after I set up the recording equipment, Leonard's hand went right underneath my skirt. I said, "What are you doing?" and he said, "This is the real dialogue," or something to that effect. I said, "Well, aside from the physical thing is there any other dialogue?" He said, "It can only be expressed in poetry." So I asked the most mundane things just to see how far the poetry would go, like "When do you get up in the morning? What did you have for breakfast? Are you happily married?" and he answered everything with poems that he had not published.'"[12]

One could parse this brief story at length: Marom's careful use of the term "whimsical" for an interaction that was in fact objectionable between a "star" and a reporter. How Marom reports Leonard's hand going under her skirt, as if the hand were independent and disembodied from the man. Her question: "Are you happily married?" One of the most telling details is how Leonard turned the interview into a game, how he wanted only his poetry and his actions to represent him. However masterful his performance, one simply cannot escape the arrogance and privilege this encounter portrays.

Forty years after his encounter with Marom, after the crash and the slow resurrection of his career, after Mount Baldy, and after years of drugs, depression, therapy, and religion, Leonard was an old man.

> I don't need a reason
> For what I became
> I've got these excuses
> They're tired and lame
> I don't need a pardon
> There's no one left to blame
> *I'm leaving the table*
> *I'm out of the game*[13]

Decades later, as an old man, it was still his poetry that Leonard wanted to represent him, despite the fact that his behaviour had become less selfish, his conduct more respectful of others. His poetry had similarly changed, becoming more obviously about death, regret, hope, and forgiveness than sexual conquest. Leonard writes so much about regret with a capital "R" that we are left to assume his personal regrets are in line. In interviews from these last days, he consistently emphasizes his gratefulness.[14]

Certainly, Leonard knew that the recovery of his career was due in large part to others, and to the fact that his legacy had already taken hold of a large community. The 1991 release of the tribute album *I'm Your Fan: The Songs of Leonard Cohen*, paved the way for his renaissance.[15] Thanks to his friends and admirers, Leonard had a rare opportunity to remake and redeem himself. He did not waste it.

Paul managed something similar when he wrote what may have been his own "farewell album": his letter to the Christ-followers at Rome. (There are several letters written after Romans that claim to be his, but historians are in wide agreement that Romans was the last

Pauline epistle that is not pseudonymous.)[16] In Romans, Paul picks up many of the same themes he wrote about to the Galatians. But whereas he was angry, vengeful, and cryptic in the earlier letter, in the later missive to Rome he is gracious – even surprisingly self-effacing:

> Bless those who persecute you; bless and do not curse them.
> Rejoice with those who rejoice, weep with those who weep.
> Live in harmony with one another;
> Do not be haughty, but associate with the lowly;
> Do not claim to be wiser than you are.
> Do not repay anyone evil for evil,
> But take thought for what is noble in the sight of all.[17]

Romans occasionally reads like a last will and testament. If so, it's a good one, and fitting for an apostle who devoted his life to peoples he did not know. The end of Paul's life is shrouded in mystery. We know he was martyred. There are traditions and myths about the details, but it seems unlikely – impossible, even – that Paul ever had the chance in his own lifetime to see his reputation recovered the way Leonard did. Tragic as that may seem, the Paul we meet in his letters would not have cared. If we take him at his word, he looked forward to the only judgment that counted for him, the judgment of his God.

———

The term "canon" refers to an authoritative collection. The word is often used of the Bible. It can also refer to any set of writings or films. There's a canon of *Sherlock Holmes* books, for instance, and a much-disputed canon of authentic *Star Trek* films and series.

For the ongoing relevance of both Leonard and of Paul, canon is important. Even before their deaths, both tried to make sure their works formed such a "canon." Paul wrote:

Greet all the brothers and sisters with a holy kiss.
I solemnly command you by the Lord that this letter be read
    to all of them.[18]

The fact that Paul wanted his letters publicly read and re-read is probably what made them among the earliest Jesus-movement documents to be collected. This, despite the fact that the historical Paul would have been dismayed that Christ's return was so delayed there even *was* a collection.

Throughout his life, Leonard did something similar. He contributed to and interacted with the fan website www.leonardcohenfiles.com maintained by Jarkko Arjatsolo. After his death, his son Adam and family and friends helped establish the Unified Heart Productions Foundation in his honour.[19] By the end of his life, Leonard knew his writings would live on; he himself had helped ensure it.

In any collection, especially one that maintains a base of fans or readers, a kind of intertextual[20] conversation goes on between present and past works. New works echo and repurpose previous or external works; words and phrases pop up again and again. In the song "Crazy to Love You," which Leonard co-wrote with Anjani Thomas, the line that he "had to do time in the tower" refers to his "Tower of Song."[21] In "You Got Me Singing," Leonard admits: "You got me singing the Hallelujah hymn," referring to his immensely popular and oft-covered Hallelujah.[22] Similarly, Paul adapted the same baptismal formula behind 1 Corinthians 12:13 when he dictated Galatians 3:28, and references biblical figures like Abraham and Hagar while talking to non-Jews for whom these were not typically ancestral figures.

Just as the fact of a collection influences the author, it also influences the reader and listener. Whether it's Shakespeare, Ian Fleming, or Leonard's discography, once there is a recognized canon, how we read, watch, or listen to works in that canon tends to operate in certain ways. Inevitably, we take one or two works as the "lens" through which we see and judge others. The result is that in a set of collected works we tend to understand the artist – or the apostle – through those pieces we consider to be the best. With Paul it might be his letter to the Romans. With Leonard, perhaps "Anthem."

If you are a Cohen fan, you may disagree with my choice of "Anthem." Those who love Leonard's work might well choose "Closing Time," or even "Democracy is Coming" as his best works. My point is that very few fans would choose a less popular piece such as "Memories" from *Death of a Ladies' Man*.[23] We choose what in our opinion makes the artist greatest. For the reader or the fan, the whole of the oeuvre is much greater than the sum of its parts.

So it is with Paul. Our evidence from the historical Paul is remarkably fragmentary and disparate. Because of the long history of Christian reception, the *remembered* Paul has always been not only deeper but also more cohesive than the evidence from his handful of genuine letters attests. As with Leonard, everything Paul composed is read through his best (or at least most popular) interpreters, and his best material. Paul's "Hallelujah" is perhaps 1 Corinthians 13, including these lines:

Love is patient; love is kind;
Love is not envious or boastful or arrogant or rude.
It does not insist on its own way; it is not irritable or resentful;
It does not rejoice in wrongdoing, but rejoices in the truth.
It bears all things, believes all things, hopes all things, en-
    dures all things.
Love never ends.[24]

These words shine so powerfully through the ages that they are still read at almost every Christian wedding. Ironically, that practice is proof of how important writings not only endure, but *change in meaning*: in light of the coming Day of the Lord, the original (as opposed to remembered) Paul actually discouraged getting married.[25] Unfortunately, misreadings of Paul have been more the rule than the

exception, and rarely have they been so benign as using 1 Corinthians
13 at weddings. At the beginning of this book, I pointed out how it
was precisely Christian misunderstandings concerning Paul's words
about Torah and about other Jews that have contributed to the long
and murderous Christian history of anti-Judaism.

Fortunately, great art and literature has an ability to change in more
positive directions as well. At its best, a writer's words can continue
to inspire *more* art and literature. Four years after Leonard's death, in
December 2020, the public art project *Cité Memoire* began to project
images onto buildings throughout Montreal. One of the most striking
was Iara Mandyn's homage to *Suzanne*. Video clips of a dreamy un-
derwater dance were projected by Michel Lemieux and Victor Pilon
against the Old Port clocktower. That tower stands close by the place
where decades before, the young Cohen was fed tea and oranges.[26]

Within a century of his death, Paul's letters were also being co-
opted in radically different ways.[27] Think of this as an ancient form
of fanfiction.[28] As mentioned in chapter 4, most biblical scholars are
certain that 1 and 2 Timothy, Ephesians, and Titus, and probably
Colossians, were *not* written by Paul, but by later followers in his
name. By the end of the first century, the circumstances in which
Paul had worked had drastically changed. The Jerusalem temple had
been destroyed by Roman troops, the Jesus movement had become
primarily non-Jewish, and Christ had not returned as predicted.
When the end of the word did not materialize as expected, unknown
Christians, faced with the prospects of longer-term survival, began to
domesticate Paul's urgent, apocalyptic words to fit into the post-war
anti-Judaism and the patriarchal gender roles and family structures of
wider Roman society. By the time of the Pastoral letters, the female
Christ-followers whom Paul advised not to marry in 1 Corinthians are
instead commanded to be obedient to husband and household and are
told that "a woman will be saved through childbearing."[29]

At the same time as this scrambling to accommodate to Roman
social mores was going on, another wing of the movement was taking

Paul's legacy in a very different direction. If you can, find and read an ancient text called the *Acts of Paul and Thecla*. It's a fascinating novel written in the second century. Thecla is a rich and beautiful urban elite woman – think *Sex in the (Roman) City*. After hearing Paul preach, Thecla is converted to the ascetic side of the Jesus movement. She turns her back on her high-class fiancé and on having children. This does not go over well. For the rest of the story, Thecla is pursued by her former fiancé and by various civic authorities, all intent on revenge. She escapes several attempts to murder her (her own mother is in on the first). In an arena where she is to be eaten by wild animals, she instead baptizes herself and escapes. Ultimately, she is honoured by God for her bravery, her perpetual celibacy, and her unwillingness to bend to social norms, and Paul gives her his blessing to work as a preacher.

These contrasting examples show the very different ways in which Paul's legacy was taken after his death. The Pastoral letters smoothed out Paul's eschatological emphases and instead adapted them to mainstream Roman society with its emphases on patriarchy and the importance of having children. In contrast, *Paul and Thecla* held on to Paul's asceticism and his (relatively) gender-levelling discipleship, as signs of the end of time.

Of the two divergent receptions of Paul, it was the misogynistic, anti-ascetic approach, accommodating to Roman pressures, that was incorporated into the New Testament. The egalitarian, mystical, and ascetic impulses that Paul set in motion continued, however, to be influential, if in more minor ways. Monasticism of both women and men, women's patronage of biblical and theological study and reform, and female mystics and leaders from Hildegard of Bingen to Dorothy Day show that the historical Paul's more radical faith continued to make converts through the centuries.[30]

As for Leonard's legacy: many adaptations of Leonard's "Hallelujah" stray just as far from the original as the Pastorals do from Paul. Too many rewrites of the song ignore Leonard's ambiguity – their saccharine lyrics are far from the demanding God, the Judaism, and the sly eroticism of Leonard's original(s). Of course, versions of "Hallelujah" represent only a small fraction of the ways Leonard continues to be mined in new work, including this book. Only time will tell how his influence on music, poetry – and, I would argue, worship – will evolve.[31] To my mind, "Come Healing" is absolutely a song of worship. Others may disagree. But by being intentionally ambiguous, Leonard designed his texts to speak beyond themselves. It is in the nature of good poetry, and good songwriting, for new audiences to continue to find themselves in the author's words.

This leads to another characteristic of great writing, lyric or otherwise. In Paul we see how a text, even one thousands of years old, can continually open itself up to new dilemmas and preoccupations. The power of Paul lies not only in how his letters spoke to his own time and place, but as Elizabeth Castelli states, how these texts now "speak beyond themselves."[32] For example, Paul's writings were used to argue both for and against the trans-Atlantic trade in enslaved persons. Ultimately, his letters proved instrumental to abolition. This despite the fact that in the first century, Paul almost certainly couldn't imagine a human society without enslavement, although he did imagine a paradise without it. In our own day, "Paul within Judaism" readings of his letters are beginning to have a positive effect as part of the wider struggle against Christian anti-Semitism.

One final irony should be pointed out: the works of both Leonard and Paul will continue to find their place in history, even though both men wrote about the *end* of history. Each was profound, in part, because he imagined the end of life as we know it. Paul imagined the collective end and Leonard dwelt on the individual end. Each brought an eternal perspective to his work. It was the God of their scriptures (differently imagined by each writer) that provided this perspective.

What lies beyond our projects, our squabbles, our hopes and fears, successes and failures? Leonard might answer: the light that shines through the cracks in everything. Paul might answer: the light we shall soon see face-to-face.

Paul was an eschatological and apocalyptic preacher. Arguably, Leonard was not – or at least, not consistently. But his constant references to courage and hope ("Democracy is Coming") in the face of death and loss turned his words in the same direction, as did his poetic disputations with the God of his scriptures.[33] Paul expected the end of society as we know it; he felt there was no point having children because of the imminent Day of the Lord. Leonard never expected such an end to society; he worked hard to leave an estate to his children. But it was precisely because Leonard knew how fleeting success could be, and how fickle human love, that he could write about divine mercy and divine judgment that speak to us above and beyond history.

Did I just write that about Leonard? It could have been Paul.

Sometimes the two sound the same eschatological notes. In words reminiscent of Paul's message (and perhaps autobiographical), Leonard warns us against losing sight of the divine apocalypse amid the riches and the cares of the world:

Naked running through the mansion
The boy with news of the Messiah
Forgets the message for his father,
Enjoying the marble against his feet.[34]

Paul adds his own warnings, words that ring through the ages:

What I am saying, brothers and sisters, is this:
flesh and blood cannot inherit the kingdom of God,
nor does the perishable inherit the imperishable. Listen, I will
    tell you a mystery!
We will not all die, but we will all be changed,
in a moment,
in the twinkling of an eye.[35]

Both wrote about what it means to live under a harsh and specific obligation to the divine. Like siblings, these two shared a family. They did so even though their personalities, their thoughts, and their ways of expressing themselves sometimes radically differed. Paul, the elder, more awkward brother, the more strident, direct, and prone to action, died not knowing the effect his words would have. Leonard, the smooth-talking romantic, the successful younger brother, prone to addiction and depression, lived long enough to see in his own days a welcome redemption, a prodigal homecoming in which he was showered with love. Paul died a martyr without realizing he would have any effect on his world at all. Leonard could see his canonization within his lifetime.

Paul's final written words are direct, to the point, and, typically, in the form of a blessing: "The God of peace be with all of you. Amen."[36] There is no doubt that Leonard chose the last lines of poetry in his final book of poetry, *The Flame* to be *his* final words. Typically, they tell a story rather than prescribing anything. Also typically, they're slightly tongue in cheek, pointing to beauty and to darkness at one and the same time. They, too, are a blessing, and a good place to end this book:

I remember him

Didn't he live
on an island in
the Mediterranean sea
with a mandate from God
to enter the dark[37]

TEXT MEDITATION

Listen to: "You Got Me Singing," *Popular Problems* (2014) and "Thanks for the Dance," *Thanks for the Dance* (2019; music Anjani Thomas).

Compare these two summary texts from Leonard and Paul:

> Thanks for the dance
> It's been hell, it's been swell,
> It's been fun
> Thanks for all the dances
> One two three, one two three one
> > ("Thanks for the Dance," *The Flame*, 103)

> I know what it is to have little
> And I know what it is to have plenty
> In any and all circumstances
> I have learned the secret of being well-fed and of going hungry,
> Of having plenty and of being in need.
> I can do all things through him who strengthens me.
> In any case, it was kind of you to share my distress.
> > (Philippians 4:12–14)

FURTHER READING

The works of great (and fortunate) artists and writers live on after they die. These works can sometimes be interpreted quite differently from the original intentions of the authors, insofar as one can even discern those intentions. This constant process of interpretation and reinterpretation is sometimes called "the life of the text" or more commonly, "reception history." An excellent treatment of how music can fit into this is Christopher Partridge's *The Lyre of Orpheus*.

On my comment about worship uses for Cohen's lyrics, and on Leonard's possible long-term significance as a writer of sacred texts, see Freedman, *Leonard Cohen: The Mystical Roots of Genius*, "Epilogue – A Modern-Day *Paytan*?"

Readers may be surprised at how "time-sensitive" I describe Paul's message to be. In fact, the delay of the *Parousia* (the expected appearance of Christ as messiah to the whole world) is central to the Christian part of the Bible. It may not be too much of an overstatement to insist that the New Testament would not exist without that anxiety. It's the reason for the existence of the canonical four gospels. Matthew and Luke, for instance, go beyond Mark to incorporate Q (an early list of Jesus's sayings), in order to pass on the message of Jesus to future generations once they realized the end had not come immediately, as expected. The delay of Jesus's return is likely behind the pre-Pauline mission to non-Palestinian Jews. It certainly was behind Paul's mission to the non-Jews, as he himself points out in Romans 9–11. The Gospel of John, on the other hand, spiritualizes or makes metaphorical the return of Christ, which is another way of addressing the delay. The New Testament's so called general letters and the pastoral epistles set up sustainable institutional hierarchies for the church, and do so in direct response to the delay of the *Parousia*. The final book in the New Testament, Revelation, was likely written earlier than many other New Testament books; like Paul's letters, it reaffirms a belief that Christ will soon return, and conveys the urgency of that return in determining the actions of followers. You can read more in Goff's "The Mystery of God's Wisdom, the Parousia of a Messiah, and Visions of Heavenly Paradise."

It is not just Paul who was an eschatological prophet. Cohen refers to this "last day" more than once in his poems and lyrics as well. For instance, I recommend reading "Beside the Shepherd," from *Let Us Compare Mythologies*.

For Jews, the question of how to remain Jewish and to thrive in a non-Jewish world is hardly new. Many of Leonard's first published poems in *Let Us Compare Mythologies* show that already at the age of twenty-one, the young man from Westmount was thinking deeply about the mix of cultures that formed him. Given his ambitions, he was also likely thinking about how he would adjust to the international stage where he soon hoped to make his mark. If you can, get a copy of this book. Spend some time with the poem "The Song of the Hellenist." In a short but powerful piece that brings together allusions to the Maccabees and to poetry by T.S. Eliot, the young Leonard compares the challenges of adapting to elite non-Jewish society with the experiences of Hellenized Jews in the second century BCE. It would be an interesting scholarly work to set this poem in place against some historical work on that period. Scholars and teachers of late Second-Temple Judaism could do worse than assigning Cohen's "Song of the Hellenist" as an exercise to undergraduate students. Even if you're not a student or scholar of the ancient world, you'll find much to reflect on.

Notes

CHAPTER ONE

1 Cohen and Layton were friends, but took different approaches to the themes described in this book. In "Irving and Me at the Hospital," in *Book of Longing*, 205, Leonard writes about Layton: "He stood up for Nietzsche / I stood up for Christ / He stood up for victory / I stood up for less."

2 The National Film Board of Canada's documentary *Ladies and Gentlemen: Mr Leonard Cohen* (1965), is ample proof that even the young Leonard had the dry wit and timing of an accomplished stand-up comic.

3 Bloom, "The Darker Side of Leonard Cohen."

4 Freedman, *Leonard Cohen*, 105–44.

5 See Erens, "Old Ideas," 198.

6 "Born in Chains," *The Flame*, 138–9.

7 Simmons, *I'm Your Man*, 506.

8 *The Flame*, 165. Like many Jews, Cohen uses the spelling G-d for "God" as both a sign of respect and a way of avoiding any possible misuse of the sacred name.

9 See Engels, "From the Dark Green Hill," 117.

10 Gilmore, "Leonard Cohen: Remembering the Life and Legacy."

11 Schneller, "Leonard Cohen's Tales of Seduction."

12 Ibid.

13 Bloom, "The Darker Side of Leonard Cohen."

14 While "apostle" is in this book's title and I use it throughout for Paul, in his own lifetime and immediately after, it was a title Paul testily claimed for himself while others denied it of him. Even the book of Acts, while giving much space to Paul and his travels, seems reluctant to label him "apostle."

15 "Cohen" is Hebrew for priest.

16 Galatians 5:12. Please note that the normal convention (and my own usual practice) when quoting the Bible is not to use footnotes but to give chapter and verse within the text itself. I am not following this convention here for a simple reason: using footnotes for Paul's writings allows for a more even comparison with Leonard's. The point of the book is to analyze their works

together, as pieces of poetic writing. All biblical quotations are from the New Revised Standard Version.

17 Romans 15:20.

18 See, for instance, Philippians 2:20–1.

19 1 Corinthians 13:13.

20 There are no physical descriptions of Paul in early documents, except for a few lines in the apocryphal *Acts of Paul and Thecla*. These gave rise to the usual image of a small, balding, intense man that we know from later Christian portrayals. Isaac Soon argues that circumstantial evidence from a number of sources may support this image of Paul, in "The Short Apostle," 159–78.

21 This is part of the reason Paul goes to such lengths to emphasize that his status as an apostle came straight from his vision of Christ and not from "human authorities": Galatians 1:1; see also 1 Corinthians 9:1–6. Acts 13:1–3 does not specify apostleship, and in any case was written much later, decades after Paul's death. For the first few centuries of Christianity, Paul appears to have been known more as a martyr than as an apostle.

22 "Going Home," *The Flame*, 107.

23 Cohen specifically mentions Paul in the title track of *The Future*, 1992; see also *Stranger Music*, 372. The reference is not positive: Cohen's dystopic vision lumps Paul in with Stalin as someone who inspires despots and murderers.

24 Gager, *Reinventing Paul*, 3.

25 Because of their familiarity to readers, I have usually limited myself to the poetry found in Cohen's lyrics. Occasionally, however, I use some of his other writing. "To know Cohen's music alone is not to know the fullness of the man's art – is really not even to know the fullness of the music," states Erens, "Old Ideas," 198.

26 When biographer Sylvie Simmons looks for reasons for Leonard's ending one of his first serious relationships, she quotes his novel *The Favourite Game* as if the protagonist's thoughts about marriage are his. See Simmons, *I'm Your Man*, 61.

27 Posner, "That's How the Light Gets In," 515.

28 *The Flame*, 208.

29 "If It Be Your Will" is a notable example, often sung by Leonard as a prayer in his concerts. See Pleshoyano, "La poésie lyrique de Leonard Cohen," 165. Pleshoyano is a Quebec academic who has extensively studied Cohen's spirituality, and who is thanked in the acknowledgements of *The Flame* for assistance with the manuscript. A moving example of Paul's language moving into prayer can be found in the final verses of 1 Corinthians 15. See also Rohter, "On the Road," 2.

30 Both tapped into the archetypical clusters of connotations and themes that, according to Canadian literary critic Northrop Frye, biblical language readily conjures among audiences influenced by Jewish (and later Christian) sacred texts. See Frye, *The Great Code*.

31 "Born in Chains," *The Flame*, 138–9; and Freedman, *Leonard Cohen*, chapter 5 "Prayer."

32 "Out of Egypt" is a reference to the book of Exodus. "First fruits" references the Jewish festival of Shavu'ot, which for Christians became Pentecost.

33 For more on this, see Castelli, *Imitating Paul*, 112.

34 Jackson, "The Prophetic Mr. Cohen."

35 Galatians 1:11.

36 *The Flame*, 159.

37 Simmons, *I'm Your Man*, 35.

38 Paul scholars debate his education in general, and specifically whether he had any formal training in rhetoric. See Harrill, *Paul the Apostle*, 24–5. For a caution see Anderson, *Ancient Rhetorical Theory and Paul*, 288–92.

39 Castelli, *Imitating Paul*, 116–17.

40 While this term may sound strange, scholars do not use the word "church" when speaking of Jesus-following communities in the first century. "Church" comes with too many anachronistic connotations. Instead, concepts like "assemblies," "Christ-assemblies," "Jesus-communities," or simply "communities" are better representations of the Greek *ekklesia* that gets rendered as "church" in English New Testaments.

41 Simmons, *I'm Your Man*, 67.

42 2 Corinthians 10:10.

43 Lebold, "Existential Troubadour to Crooner of Light," 2.

44 Marchal, *Appalling Bodies*, 1.

45 Eisenbaum, *Paul Was Not a Christian*, 35–6.

46 "Light as the Breeze," *Stranger Music*, 375–6.

47 1 Corinthians 7:7.

48 Gilmore, "Leonard Cohen: Remembering the Life and Legacy."

49 Lebold, "Existential Troubadour to Crooner of Light," 3.

50 1 Corinthians 7:5–7.

51 Bloom, "The Darker Side of Leonard Cohen."

52 Among the thousands of examples, one of my favourites is "Because of a Few Songs," in *Book of Longing*, 208. Simmons writes that, at adolescence, Cohen learned hypnosis, which he immediately put to use by hypnotizing the family's young maid into taking off her clothes. Simmons, *I'm Your Man*, 19.

53 Romans 15:16. On the importance of the name and position "cohen," see
   Freedman, *Leonard Cohen*, 218–21.

54 Donald Grayston employs a somewhat similar technique to compare Cohen
   and Thomas Merton. See "Monastic in His Own Way, 3–9.

55 In "Monastic in His Own Way," 7, Grayston states that Cohen burst "the
   bonds of cultural constraint which for the most part confine poetry to a
   limited audience and monasticism to its institutional base."

56 Simmons, *I'm Your Man*, 481.

57 Ibid., 55–6.

58 A.M. Klein, "The Bible as Literature," in *Literary Essays and Reviews*, 129.

59 "Almost Like the Blues," *The Flame*, 127.

CHAPTER TWO

1 Freedman, *Leonard Cohen*, 211, 218.

2 Devlin, *Leonard Cohen: In His Own Words*, 7.

3 Posner notes that "Rabbi Solomon Klonitzky-Kline was known as the Sar
   HaDikduki (master of grammarians) and wrote (among several other works)
   a thesaurus on Talmudic interpretation," "That's How the Light Gets In," 512.

4 On the relationship between his Buddhism and Judaism, see Cohen, "One of My
   Letters," *Book of Longing*, 5. On Sufi imagery, see Freedman, *Leonard Cohen*, 211.

5 Engels, "From the Dark Green Hill," 118.

6 Devlin, *Leonard Cohen: In His Own Words*, 26.

7 Simmons, *I'm Your Man*, 315, 508. See also O'Neil, "Leonard Cohen: Singer of
   the Bible," 98–9.

8 Curnyn, "Leonard Cohen, Religious Alchemist."

9 "Not a Jew," *Book of Longing*, 158.

10 Philippians 3:5.

11 Harrill, *Paul the Apostle*, 26–31; Eisenbaum, *Paul Was Not a Christian*, 66.
   Judaism in the first century (and since) is hardly the undifferentiated entity
   Christians have historically assumed, usually for polemical purposes.

12 Novenson lists both admirers and critics who incorrectly assume Paul's
   break from Judaism in "Did Paul Abandon," 240.

13 Eisenbaum, *Paul Was Not a Christian*, 142–3. See Fredriksen, *Paul: The
   Pagan's Apostle*, 108–9, for a brief summary of the historical development of
   this interpretation.

14 Doering, "Early Judaism and Early Christianity," 543–4.

15 Ibid., 547–50.

16 Among others, these books are useful for learning more about misinterpretations of Paul and anti-Judaism: Luther, Schramm, and Stjerna, *Martin Luther, the Bible, and the Jewish People*, 2012, and Probst, *Demonizing the Jews: Luther and the Protestant Church in Nazi Germany*, 2012.

17 Fredriksen, "If It Looks Like a Duck," 25–33.

18 Galatians 1:15.

19 The recalcitrant prophet Jonah famously attempted to hide from God on a ship, only to be dragged back to shore in the belly of a fish to bring God's message to the people of Ninevah (Jonah 1:1–2:10).

20 On Paul's interpretation of his scriptures as midrash, Rosen-Zvi, "Early Judaism and Rabbinic Judaism," 496–7.

21 Email from Leonard Cohen to Peter Dale Scott. From Cohen, *The Flame*, 159.

22 Simmons, *I'm Your Man*, 7. Occasionally, Leonard would sign with all three names – Jewish, Buddhist, and "Christian."

23 Freedman, *Leonard Cohen*, 1, points out that Eliezer (Lazarus) was Cohen's great-grandfather's name, and that Leonard was named for him. Typical of Leonard, the name reflected multiple heritages at the same time.

24 It's worth noting that this was not the case for Jesus, who spoke Aramaic, and is reported as travelling in a very small area among the villages and towns of the Galilee. Jesus never seems to have strayed far from his semi-agrarian roots, except to go on pilgrimage to Jerusalem, where he was murdered.

25 On cosmopolitanism, see Ascough, *Lydia, Paul's Cosmopolitan Hostess*, 12, and Neutel, *A Cosmopolitan Ideal*.

26 "The Song of the Hellenist," in *Let Us Compare Mythologies*, 4.

27 Ascough, *Lydia, Paul's Cosmopolitan Hostess*, 22.

28 On Cohen's ongoing Jewish identity see Mus and Trehearne, *The Demons of Leonard Cohen*, 150–1.

29 Wieseltier, "My Friend Leonard Cohen."

30 Simmons, *I'm Your Man*, 438, quotes Leonard on similarities between "God's creative activity" in the Kabbalah and in the Roshi's teachings.

31 Caputo and Alcoff, *St. Paul among the Philosophers*; Engberg-Pedersen, *Paul and the Stoics*.

32 1 Corinthians 9:22.

33 *Stranger Music*, 347. On the circumstances of writing "Hallelujah," see Simmons, *I'm Your Man*, 319–21 and 328–30.

34 "Love Itself," *Book of Longing*, 54.

35 For a summary of research on the "Parting of the Ways" between Christianity and Judaism, see Reinhartz, "A Fork in the Road?", 280–95, and Donaldson, *Gentile Christian Identity*, 37–54.

36 Curnyn, "Leonard Cohen, Religious Alchemist."

37 Interesting in this regard is Cohen, "The Future," *Stranger Music*, 371: "I'm the little jew / who wrote the bible."

38 See Galatians 2:9, where Paul writes: "And when James and Cephas and John, who were acknowledged pillars, recognized the grace that had been given to me, they gave to Barnabas and to me the right hand of fellowship, agreeing that we should go to the Gentiles and they to the circumcised."

39 1 Thessalonians 1:9.

40 The ancient world was crowded with divine and semi-divine beings who were believed to affect every part of daily life, and who guarded "their" followers jealously in familial groupings. Paul's message upset this balance. See Fredriksen, *Paul: The Pagan's Apostle*, 89–90. See also Cohen's poem "The Embrace," *Stranger Music*, 396–7.

41 1 Thessalonians 1:9–10.

42 Donaldson, *Gentile Christian Identity*, 159. For a summary (based on prior work by Donaldson) see Thiessen, *Paul and the Gentile Problem*, 20–4.

43 On ancient Jewish debates about whether gentiles could convert to Judaism (and thus on what constitutes Jewish identity) see Thiessen, *Contesting Conversion*, 86. Also Fredriksen, *Paul, the Pagan's Apostle*, 74–77.

44 Adapted from Ehrman, *The New Testament: A Historical Introduction*, 495.

45 Thiessen, *Paul and the Gentile Problem*, 26 and 32.

46 Among others, Gager, *Reinventing Paul*, 18. See Romans 11:1; 2 Corinthians 11:22; but also see 2 Corinthians 3.

47 For instance, Romans 3:19-20; 9:8; 11:7, etc.

48 Fredriksen, *Paul, The Pagan's Apostle*, 114. For helpful nuancing of Fredriksen's position, see McDonald, "Ex-Pagan Pagans?" and Joshua D. Garroway, "Paul: Within Judaism, Without Law."

49 For succinct summaries of the "perspectives on Paul" see Doering, *Early Judaism and Early Christianity*, 547–50, and Anderson, "Judeophobia and Pauline Scholarship," (in publication).

50 Gager, *Reinventing Paul*, 14.

51 For a rather charitable treatment of Martin Luther and the misappropriation of Paul, see Eisenbaum, *Paul Was Not a Christian*, 48–54.

52 Jackson, "The Prophetic Mr. Cohen."

53 Burger and Hahn, *Leonard Cohen on Leonard Cohen*, 4; see also Cohen, "August 2, 1976," *The Flame*, 262: "I stole your savior."

54 On the connection between these lines and the patriarch Jacob, see Freedman, *Leonard Cohen*, 96–7.

CHAPTER THREE

1   Galatians 2:20.
2   Devlin, *Leonard Cohen: In His Own Words*, 11. See also Freedman, *Leonard Cohen*, 115–16, 140.
3   "For Wilf and His House," in *Let Us Compare Mythologies*, 2.
4   Simmons, *I'm Your Man*, 23.
5   See Gauvreau, *The Catholic Origins*.
6   Simmons, *I'm Your Man*, 56.
7   Devlin, *Leonard Cohen: In His Own Words*, 10; Freedman, *Leonard Cohen*, 140.
8   "Ballad," *Let Us Compare Mythologies*, 31. To my mind this is a stronger example of the young Leonard's use of crucifixion imagery than "For Wilf and His House," which is more often quoted.
9   Devlin, *Leonard Cohen: In His Own Words*, 37.
10 *The Flame*, 268.
11 Nicolet-Anderson, "Cohen, Leonard."
12 O'Brian, "Songs and Thoughts of Leonard Cohen."
13 Horrell, *Introduction*, 28–30.
14 1 Corinthians 2:2 and 8.
15 "Another Christopher," *Book of Longing*, 132.
16 Henze, "Apocalyptic Literature," 422.
17 1 Corinthians chapter 7. Paul seems to have assumed that marital bonds, along with other societal structures like enslavement (endemic in the Roman world), would be dissolved in the new order and the Day of the Lord. Although his thinking about this event evolved over his surviving letters, it remained a focal point throughout.
18 1 Thessalonians 1:10; 1 Corinthians 15:24–5.
19 It is ironic that while much within Paul's letters was occasional and meant to be temporary, the letters have become the soil from which so much commentary has grown, while Leonard consciously wrote his lyrics to have multiple layers of meaning and deep allusion, yet his lyrics are enjoyed by so many in an ephemeral way.
20 Philippians 4:5, 1 Corinthians 7:29 and 31, 1 Corinthians 10:11, and 1 Corinthians 15:51–2 among others.
21 2 Corinthians 5:16–17. Those translations which use the term "he" add it where it did not exist in the Greek. In the Greek, the statement could almost as easily be translated as something like "if anyone (as in even one person) is in Christ, there is a new creation (that is, the new order of resurrection has begun)."

22 Romans 6:3. None of Paul's letters are dated, so their relative chronology is educated guesswork. But many scholars feel that Romans is the last surviving letter of Paul's. Note that he wrote other letters that did not survive (see 1 Corinthians 5:9).

23 Philippians 1:21.

24 "Show Me the Place," *The Flame*, 111. Given Cohen's penchant for fusing the erotic and the spiritual, Simmons, *I'm Your Man*, 493, says that "the words might as easily be addressed to a naked woman as to an Old Testament God." I do not agree with Cohen's biographer here. Freedman, *Leonard Cohen*, 32, argues that these lyrics refer to Jacob rolling the stone from the mouth of the well in Haran (Genesis 29:10). However, the lyric "where the Word became a man" indicates a likely overlaying by Cohen of the stories of the resurrection of Jesus in addition. Such multivalent, overlapping, meaning is typical of both Leonard and the Bible.

25 Nicolet-Anderson, "Cohen, Leonard" writes that "One comes out of the song 'Amen' with a sense that it might be human beings who are better suited in their brokenness to heal the divine."

26 See 1 Corinthians 1:23.

27 "Israel," *Stranger Music*, 323–4. See also the Jacob reference in Cohen, "The Drunk Is Gender Free," *Book of Longing*, 143.

28 See "Prayer for the Messiah," *Let Us Compare Mythologies*, 6.

29 Philippians 2:9.

30 Engels, "From the Dark Green Hill," 118.

31 Nicolet-Anderson, "Leonard Cohen's Use of the Bible," 227.

32 This was established by Marguerite Bourgeoys in 1678 as a pilgrimage church for the early French settlement. In "Suzanne," Cohen plays with the identity of "our lady of good help." Freedman, *Leonard Cohen*, 114–15, suggests an apocryphal Christian legend that may have informed "Suzanne."

33 "Suzanne," *Stranger Music*, 95.

34 Nicolet-Anderson, "Leonard Cohen's Use of the Bible," 227.

35 Leonard once quipped, "Any guy who says 'Blessed are the poor, Blessed are the meek' has got to be a figure of unparalleled generosity and insight and madness." Devlin, *Leonard Cohen: In His Own Words*, 11.

36 Philippians 2:9–11. Over the centuries since, many Christians have forgotten that Jesus was to have been the first of the resurrection of all humans, not someone undergoing a unique event.

37 "The Stranger Song," *Stranger Music*, 111–12.

38 On this, see Mus and Trehearne, *The Demons of Leonard Cohen*, 153.

39 On Paul's surprisingly high Christology, see Fredriksen, *Paul: The Pagan's Apostle*, 144–5

40 1 Corinthians 15:25, 26, and 28.

41 The prophetic books of the Hebrew Bible refer to the concept frequently, e.g. Isaiah 2:12; Ezekiel 13:5; Joel 3:14; Amos 5:18–20; Obadiah 15; Zephaniah 1:7; Zechariah 14:1; Malachi 4:5. Paul picks it up in several letters, including 1 Corinthians 5:5; 2 Corinthians 1:14; and 1 Thessalonians 5:2. Freedman, *Leonard Cohen*, 226–7 shows how Cohen's use of legends concerning Jerusalem's Gate of Mercy open some interesting points of contact between Leonard and Paul's message concerning Jesus.

42 "The Tower of Song," *Stranger Music*, 363–4.

CHAPTER FOUR

1 Mus and Trehearne, *The Demons of Leonard Cohen*, 150, point out how Cohen playfully used the same Jewish writing convention that respectfully renders the deity's name as "G-d" to render the word "sex" as "s-x." In my opinion, there is a profound statement on the nature of God behind this tongue-in-cheek play.

2 Berger, "Women's Liturgical Practices and Leadership Roles," 191.

3 See Mersereau, "Great Moments in Canadian Music (Track 3): Cohen's Comeback – How a Tribute Album Revived Leonard Cohen's Career," for a brief history of Jennifer Warnes's effect on Leonard's music and career.

4 On male authors "thinking with women" in the ancient world see Parks, Sheinfeld, and Warren, *Jewish and Christian Women*, 222.

5 Lévi-Strauss, *Le Totémisme Aujourd'hui*; Peter Brown, *The Body and Society*.

6 Simmons, *I'm Your Man*, 435.

7 Bassler, "First Corinthians," 558. It is possible that social interactions at that time were often segregated by gender.

8 On this, see Lebold, "Existential Troubadour to Crooner of Light," 3.

9 "Opened My Eyes," *Book of Longing*, 156.

10 Bassler, "First Corinthians," 557–9.

11 "What I Do," *The Flame*, 54.

12 Lebold, "Existential Troubadour to Crooner of Light," 2.

13 Mus and Trehearne, *The Demons of Leonard Cohen*, 150. Also Nicolet-Anderson, "Cohen, Leonard," n.p.

14 "Leaving the Table," *You Want It Darker* (2016); *The Flame*, 150.

15 "Thing," *Book of Longing*, 112.

16 "So Long, Marianne," *Stranger Music*, 100.

17 An example is "Light as the Breeze," *Stranger Music*, 375–6, where Leonard uses images from the book of Revelation to describe oral sex.

18 Freedman, *Leonard Cohen*, 19–20.

19 Lebold, "Existential Troubadour to Crooner of Light," 2.

20 "Hallelujah," *Stranger Music*, 347.

21 See Lebold, "Existential Troubadour to Crooner of Light," 2.

22 Simmons, *I'm Your Man*, 55.

23 See, e.g., Psalm 41/42, Psalm 62/63, Psalm 83/84.

24 "Come Healing," *The Flame*, 116.

25 Nor did Leonard find happiness in a household of women only as a youth. See Simmons, *I'm Your Man*, 404.

26 Schneller, "Leonard Cohen's Tales of Seduction."

27 "Death of a Ladies' Man," *Stranger Music*, 228.

28 Philippians 4:2–3. For more on the likely ongoing relevance of women's leadership in Philippi after Paul, see Ascough, *Lydia: Paul's Cosmopolitan Hostess*, 96–9.

29 Longenecker, "Salvation History in Galatians," 65–87, Gager, *Reinventing Paul*, 10.

30 Romans 16:2.

31 Romans 16:7. For much of Christian history, the Greek "Junia" was mistranslated to a masculine name by biblical translators who simply could not (or would not) believe that a woman could be an apostle. See Brooten, "'Junia ... Outstanding among the Apostles,'" 141–4.

32 1 Corinthians 11:2–16, if authentic, seems to indicate that Paul did uphold a gender distinction in terms of attire for those leading worship, at least in the case of Corinth where decorum in worship seemed to be causing controversy.

33 Parks, in *Gender in the Rhetoric of Jesus*, demonstrates that Jesus's teaching style was deliberately inclusive of women, placing them on an identical playing field with men in terms of intellectual capacity and religious authority, not because he was different from the Judaism around him, but because he was a participant in early Jewish and late Hellenistic circles that offered more opportunities for participation to women; see especially 111–14, 122–3.

34 1 Timothy 2:11–15.

35 See Cavan W. Concannon's "Paul and Authorship."

36 For more, see Eastman, "The Pastoral Epistles."

37 There is one genuine, undisputed letter of Paul that has two passages that do not seem favourable to women's equality; 1 Corinthians has a bizarre

midrash in favour of women's head coverings in chapter 11 that argues that men are the "head" of women, and in chapter 14 it cautions women to be silent in assemblies. Because these passages are so inconsistent with the multiple pieces of evidence across Paul's authentic corpus for women in leadership (even specific instructions for what women should wear *while prophesying in the assembly*), scholars have puzzled over the two Corinthian passages, some pointing out evidence that the call to silence was a later "interpolation" (scribal addition to bring later copies of the letter in line with later Christian hierarchies) and others positing a specific disruptive situation within the Corinthian community that brought about unique advice from Paul.

38 See May, *Homeward Bound*.

39 Simmons, *I'm Your Man*, 22.

40 See D'Angelo, "Roman 'Family Values' and the Apologetic Concerns of Philo and Paul," 525–46. Also Roetzel, "Sex and the Single God," 231–48, and Ascough, *Lydia: Paul's Cosmopolitan Hostess*, 96.

41 Galatians 3:28. Due to the construction using "and," this probably refers to his ideal of no marriage, but it also moves to transcend gender as a criterion for inclusion/exclusion.

42 Freedman, *Leonard Cohen*, 21.

43 *Talmud* Kethubod 61b: "The times for conjugal duty prescribed in the Torah are: for men of independent means, every day; for laborers, twice a week; for donkey drivers, once a week; for camel drivers, once in thirty days; for sailors, once in six months." Paul is aware of this: "The husband should give to his wife her conjugal rights, and likewise the wife to her husband (1 Corinthians 7:3)."

44 1 Corinthians 7:32–4.

45 Galatians 3:28. See Neutel, *A Cosmopolitan Ideal*.

46 1 Corinthians 7:3–6.

47 Aristophanes (Symposium) and other ancients wrote about a creation time when there was only one gender which combined both male and female. It may be that Paul, in Galatians 3:28, obliquely references this belief. Notably, one of the creation stories of Genesis begins with one human being who is then "split" into male and female. Cohen alludes to this: "And Be As Adam Was To Eve / Before The Great Divide," in "Drank a Lot," *The Flame*, 73.

48 Ehrensperger, "Paul, the Man," 76.

CHAPTER FIVE

1 Mersereau, "Cohen's Comeback."

2 "Chelsea Hotel," *Stranger Music*, 197.

3 See Posner, "That's How the Light Gets In," 512. Also Freedman, *Leonard Cohen*, 21–2.

4 Castelli, "Disciplines of Difference."

5 "Early Morning at Mt. Baldy," *Book of Longing*, 21.

6 For a description of the camp and the brutal daily regimen, see Simmons, *I'm Your Man*, 377–81.

7 "The Collapse of Zen," *Book of Longing*, 20.

8 Simmons, *I'm Your Man*, 300. As psychologically interesting as they might be, to go into depth about the many motivations behind Leonard's time on Mt Baldy is beyond the subject of this book. So is his complicated personal relationship with the Roshi, whose own sexual interactions with members of the movement were purported to be abusive and deeply troubling. Leonard makes veiled reference to this in "Early Questions," *Book of Longing*, 45.

9 "My Teacher," *Stranger Music*, 322.

10 Partridge, *The Lyre of Orpheus*, 46.

11 "The Drunk Is Gender Free," *Book of Longing*, 143.

12 Simmons, *I'm Your Man*, 103, describes some of the many influences Leonard and others explored on Hydra.

13 See Boyarin, "Body Politic among the Brides of Christ," 459–78.

14 See 1 Thessalonians 4:3–5: "this is the will of God, your sanctification: that you abstain from fornication; that each one of you know how to control your own body in holiness and honor, not with lustful passion, like the Gentiles who do not know God."

15 1 Corinthians 7:1, Paul does not say whether the reverse, "it is good for a woman not to touch a man," is also "good," underlining that very few women of that time had a choice in the patriarchal society of the day. This is reminiscent of the uninvited sexual contact that Simmons points out as characteristic of the younger Cohen (and of men in general in that much more recent era). See Simmons, *I'm Your Man*, 268.

16 1 Corinthians 7:7.

17 "There Are No Traitors," *Stranger Music*, 165.

18 "The Dream," *Stranger Music*, 256.

19 1 Corinthians 9:25–7. See the later comments on Paul's possible relationships to Stoicism.

20 Philippians 3:8. "Rubbish" is not a strong enough translation.

21 Philippians 4:12.

22 However, see Mark 2:18–20 and its parallels for the idea that Jesus and his disciples fasted far less than John the Baptist and his followers.

23 Acts, a later and rather heroic early Christian account of Paul, mentions his fasting at Acts 27:21, perhaps in the context of a festival (Acts 27:9).

24 Simmons, *I'm Your Man*, 104.

25 "A Limited Degree," *Book of Longing*, 65.

26 "Food Tastes Good," *Book of Longing*, 48.

27 See 1 Corinthians 8. Many scholars are convinced that the appropriateness of eating space (commensality) was also behind the conflict with Peter and the people from James that Paul mentions in Galatians 2:11–14. See Nanos, "Reading the Antioch Incident," 26–52.

28 Devlin, *Leonard Cohen: In His Own Words*, 30.

29 There are many, many examples such as, from his earlier work, "The Killers," *Stranger Music*, 176, and from his later, "Almost Like the Blues," *The Flame*, 127.

30 In the Roman Empire (as today, but even more), masculinity was performed instead of being automatic. The Roman man (*vir*) was always in danger of losing that privileged status. Neither could the enslaved persons who made up such a large percentage of the Empire's population (and a significant portion of the Christ assemblies) choose to give up (forced) sex, or food, if commanded by their masters.

CHAPTER SIX

1 An alternative translation to the NRSV's "be courageous" at 1 Corinthians 16:13.

2 Butler, *Undoing Gender*, 42–3. For an example of how Paul used feminine metaphors in his writings in service of masculine ideals and tactics, see Emmett, "The Apostle Paul's Maternal Masculinity," 15–37.

3 See chapter two of Marchal, *Appalling Bodies*.

4 See Parks, Sheinfeld, and Warren, *Jewish and Christian Women*, 229.

5 The ancient world's concept of gender was not the same as our own. Roman males achieved, maintained, and could lose, manly status through acts or failures of discipline and performance. All other persons, including women, were seen as incomplete males. Very rarely, an anatomical female could achieve the status of *vir*, just as most anatomical males (for example, the male enslaved) never achieved it. For more see Larson, "Paul's Masculinity," 85–97.

6 Ehrensperger, "Paul, the Man," 69.

7 See Conway, *Behold the Man* and Castelli, "'I Will Make Mary Male'," 29–49.

8 Stewart, "Masculinity in the New Testament and Early Christianity," 91–102. See also Ehrensperger, "Paul, the Man," 70–1.

9 See "The Faithless Wife," *Book of Longing*, 147.

10 Devlin, *Leonard Cohen: In His Own Words*, 18.

11 For example, "The Great Divide," *Book of Longing*, 191–2.

12 "My Room," *Stranger Music*, 173.

13 "Another Poet," *Book of Longing*, 186.

14 Simmons, *I'm Your Man*, 484.

15 See *Stranger Music*, 351–2.

16 Simmons, *I'm Your Man*, 9.

17 "The Traitor," *Stranger Music*, 304–5.

18 "The Warrior Boats," *Let Us Compare Mythologies*, 23–4.

19 "Field Commander Cohen," *Stranger Music*, 201.

20 "Ballad," *Let Us Compare Mythologies*, 31.

21 By contrast, Jesus as portrayed in the gospels seems to rely almost exclusively on metaphors from agriculture and village life (shepherds, farmers, birds). Paul employs urban allusions to athletes and soldiers.

22 Philippians 2:25, Philemon 2.

23 1 Corinthians 9:7.

24 It is debated by scholars whether Paul was a fully-practicing Stoic (an adherent of the ancient philosophical school), or simply relied on more general stoic ideas that permeated the culture of this time. See Caputo and Alcoff, *St. Paul Among the Philosophers*.

25 Philippians 4:11b–13.

26 National Film Board of Canada, "Ladies and Gentlemen," 1965.

27 Simmons, *I'm Your Man*, 483–4.

28 See Taylor, "Male-Female Missionary Pairings among Jesus' Disciples," 11–25.

29 There are exceptions. See "I'm Always Thinking of a Song," *The Flame*, 36.

30 "Waiting for the Miracle," *Stranger Music*, 380–1.

31 See, for example, "This is War," and "The Traitor," *Stranger Music*, 184 and 304–5.

32 Simmons, *I'm Your Man*, 356.

33 "There Are No Traitors," *Stranger Music*, 165.

34 Bloom, "The Darker Side of Leonard Cohen."

35 Parks, "Because of Her We All Die."

36 2 Corinthians 12:10.

37 Conway, *Behold the Man*. Ehrensperger, "Paul, the Man," 76.

38 See 1 Corinthians 9:24–7. Paul's assertions sometimes sound like *ad hoc* attempts to retrieve some honour from what may have been difficult, even catastrophic, interactions. (This again sounds like Leonard, at times).

39 Devlin, *Leonard Cohen: In His Own Words*, 17.

40 Lebold, "Existential Troubadour to Crooner of Light," 4. In Jewish tradition, "fear" also suggests "awe," which also describes the attitude toward women in much of Leonard's poetry.

41 "Waiting for the Miracle," *Stranger Music*, 381.

42 My thanks to Dr Sara Parks for this observation, which comes from our conversation about Cohen and Jennifer Warnes.

43 Devlin, *Leonard Cohen: In His Own Words*, 18.

44 "Days of Kindness," *Stranger Music*, 401.

45 Simmons, *I'm Your Man*, 450.

46 "So Long, Marianne," *Stranger Music*, 100.

47 In his surviving letters, Paul uses a number of feminine metaphors. Emmett, "The Apostle Paul's Maternal Masculinity," 15–37 has shown that these nonetheless work to reinforce a masculine strategy of persuasion.

48 2 Corinthians 11:1–2.

49 As a young poet, Leonard worked hard to shake off his origins in upper-class Westmount, his schooling at McGill, and his headship of a McGill fraternity.

50 Bhabha, "Of Mimicry and Man," 131.

51 1 Corinthians 9:19, 22–3.

52 "I'm Your Man," *Stranger Music*, 357–8.

CHAPTER SEVEN

1 1 Thessalonians 2:19.

2 Harris, *Ancient Literacy*, 266–8.

3 Norton, Allen, and Askin, eds, *Reading, Writing and Bookish Circles*.

4 1 Corinthians 16:1.

5 The National Film Board of Canada is an undervalued treasure for its documentation of Canada's up-and-coming artists, and they have a variety of recordings of Leonard Cohen as a budding poet. "Ladies and Gentlemen … Mr Leonard Cohen" in particular is a treat fans should not miss.

6 "Everybody Knows," *Stranger Music*, 361.

7 Cohen does this in many of his songs. See for instance "Amen," *The Flame*, 109.

8 "Hallelujah," *Stranger Music*, 347.

9   Leonard wrote some of his songs to contemporaneous or former lovers, for instance.

10 For example, "Thing," *Book of Longing*, 112.

11 "You Got Me Singing," *The Flame*, 140.

12 As pointed out years ago by Barclay, "Mirror-Reading a Polemical Letter," 73–93.

13 Galatians 3:21.

14 Chloe is yet another example of Paul's working partnerships with women.

15 1 Corinthians 1:12.

16 Gager, *Reinventing Paul*, 13.

17 Mus and Trehearne, *The Demons of Leonard Cohen*, 80.

18 For more on this, see Olbricht and Sumney, *Paul and Pathos*.

19 Seesengood, "'Not Grudgingly, nor under Compulsion,'" 145.

20 Philemon 4–6.

21 Readers interested in exploring Paul's strategies in Philemon should consult Maier, "Paul's Letter to Philemon," 530–1.

22 "My Oh My," *The Flame*, 134.

23 Philemon 21.

24 On the origins of this concept, see Lévi-Strauss, *Le Totémisme Aujourd'hui*; Peter Brown, *The Body and Society*.

25 Tolmie, "How Onesimus Was Heard – Eventually," 102.

26 "Dance Me to the End of Love," *Stranger Music*, 337–8.

27 1 Corinthians 4:11–13a.

28 Both Simmons and Shapiro discuss the song "Waiting for a Miracle" and/ or the whole album *The Future* as possible sites of romantic communication with, including a proposal of marriage to, Rebecca De Mornay. Simmons, "I'm Your Man," 356; Shapiro, "The End of the World."

29 Partridge, *The Lyre of Orpheus*, 47.

30 "Poem," *Let Us Compare Mythologies*, 44.

31 Philemon 9.

32 Galatians 2:20.

33 1 Corinthians 15:9–10.

34 "Nov 6, 2005," *The Flame*, 183.

35 1 Corinthians 2:1.

36 2 Corinthians 10:10.

37 2 Corinthians 10:17.

38 "Slow," *The Flame*, 125.

39 2 Corinthians 11:7.

40 Cohen and Thomas, "Crazy to Love You," *The Flame*, 115.

41 Freedman, *Leonard Cohen*, 204–6.

42 "Coming Back to You," *Stranger Music*, 340.

43 Philippians 2:5a.

44 "If I Didn't Have Your Love," *The Flame*, 151.

CHAPTER EIGHT

1 Devlin, *Leonard Cohen: In His Own Words*, 66.

2 "Song of Patience," *Let Us Compare Mythologies*, 15.

3 Galatians 1:15–16.

4 Seesengood, "'Not Grudgingly, nor under Compulsion,'" 141, 143.

5 "Bird on the Wire," *Stranger Music*, 144.

6 On Paul's use of Jeremiah as model, see Doering, "The Commissioning of Paul," 544–65.

7 Mus and Trehearne, *The Demons of Leonard Cohen*, 61.

8 Jackson, "The Prophetic Mr. Cohen."

9 Freedman, *Leonard Cohen*, 245.

10 "Ballad," *Let Us Compare Mythologies*, 31.

11 One of the many Cohen biographies explicitly identifies him as a "prophet": Dorman and Rawlins, *Leonard Cohen: Prophet of the Heart*.

12 Concannon, "'Not for an Olive Wreath, but Our Lives,'" 212.

13 Philippians 2:17.

14 Philippians 2:18.

15 Mus and Trehearne, *The Demons of Leonard Cohen*, 151. On Cohen's own sense of himself as a prophet, see Freedman, *Leonard Cohen*, 245.

16 Devlin, *Leonard Cohen: In His Own Words*, 23.

17 Nicolet-Anderson, "Cohen, Leonard."

18 "Amen," *The Flame*, 110.

19 "Hallelujah," *Stranger Music*, 347.

20 "Came So Far for Beauty," *Stranger Music*, 297.

21 Erens, "Old Ideas," 199.

22 "The Tower of Song," *Stranger Music*, 363.

23 1 Corinthians 9:16.

24 2 Corinthians 6:8b–10.

25 Devlin, *Leonard Cohen: In His Own Words*, 61.

26 Romans 15:32–3.

27 Freedman, *Leonard Cohen*, 238. This echoes the inverse human redemption of the divine discussed by Nicolet-Anderson.

28 "You Want It Darker," *The Flame*, 143.

29 Romans 1:1. I have changed the NRSV translations of "servant" to "slave," and
    "apostle" to "messenger." "Slave" is not only more accurate to the Greek
    doulos, it also captures the full sense of ownership, loss of self-will, and utter
    life of compulsion of an enslaved person better than our inaccurate but high-
    ly media-influenced images of "servant," informed as we are by film repre-
    sentations of nineteenth-century English butlers. There has been criticism
    of Paul for appropriating the term *doulos* as a metaphor when enslavement
    was a desperate reality for so many in the first century. I believe, however,
    that the precarity of even free but lower-class persons like Paul, and the fre-
    quency with which they could become enslaved, attenuates this criticism.
    Apostle is the usual translation of *apostolos*, or "one who is sent." Here, I
    chose messenger to allow the term's function to be better understood.
30 Read this piece in its entirety to get a better sense of Cohen's sense of calling.

CHAPTER NINE

1   Erens, "Old Ideas," 202.
2   "Ain't No Cure for Love," *Stranger Music*, 356. Here again, Leonard's lyrics
    are intentionally ambiguous and polyvalent, denoting both human (here,
    same-sex?) love and divine love at once. By contrast, Jennifer Warnes's ver-
    sion of this song seems to allude to her love for Cohen.
3   Devlin, *Leonard Cohen: In His Own Words*, 49.
4   2 Corinthians 12:1–4 edited. Emphasis added.
5   "Born in Chains," *The Flame*, 138–9.
6   1 Thessalonians 4:17.
7   Freedman *Leonard Cohen*, 116.
8   See Lieber, "Early Judaism and Mysticism," 523–4.
9   Isaiah 6:6.
10 Ezekiel 37:1–14.
11 Tobit 6.
12 Testament of Abraham, first or second century CE.
13 Freedman, *Leonard Cohen*, 187–90.
14 The Jewish tradition known as *Merkabah* (chariot) mysticism includes heav-
    enly journeys. See Avery-Peck, "Seven Heavens," 370, and Morray-Jones,
    "Paradise Revisited (2 Cor 12:1–12)," 265–92.
15 Sulzbach, "When Going on a Heavenly Journey," 164.
16 "Thousand Kisses Deep," *Book of Longing*, 56–7.
17 Nicolet-Anderson, "Cohen, Leonard."

18 Albert Schweitzer first argued this way for Paul's "Christ mysticism" in the
    1930s in *The Mysticism of Paul the Apostle*. For Schweitzer and many others in
    the twentieth century, Paul's mysticism was wrongly attributed to Greek
    influences separate from his Jewishness. For a more recent view see Du Toit,
    "'In Christ,' 'in the Spirit,' and Related Prepositional Phrases," 287–98.

19 Enslaved persons in the Roman Empire were often used for sex. Given that
    some early Christians were enslaved, ancient church writers noted that ad-
    monitions against "fornication" and "adultery" were seen as not applying to
    the enslaved when they had no choice in such activities.

20 1 Corinthians 6:15–20.

21 Mersereau, "Cohen's Comeback."

22 Mus and Trehearne, *The Demons of Leonard Cohen*, 64.

23 Devlin, *Leonard Cohen: In His Own Words*, 51.

24 "Drank a Lot," *The Flame* 74.

25 Romans 8:26.

26 Pleshoyano, "Leonard Cohen's Poiesis," 19.

27 Nicolet-Anderson, "Cohen, Leonard," n.p.

28 "August 2, 1976," *The Flame*, 263.

29 1 Corinthians 5:3–5.

30 Mus and Trehearne, *The Demons of Leonard Cohen*, 81.

31 "Going Home," *The Flame*, 107. See, however, his words in "Travelogue": "to
    the young let me say: / I am not sage, rebbe, roshi, guru / I am Bad Example."
    The Flame, 259.

32 Grayston, "Monastic in His Own Way," 5.

33 1 Corinthians 4:1.

34 "You Want It Darker," *The Flame*, 143.

35 "Banjo," *The Flame*, 118.

36 1 Thessalonians 1:10.

37 "The Night Comes On," *Stranger Music*, 346.

38 1 Corinthians 9:16b.

39 On brokenness as a theme in the Jewish Kabbalistic tradition, see Freedman,
    Leonard Cohen, 147–8.

40 Mus and Trehearne, *The Demons of Leonard Cohen*, 153.

41 Freedman, *Leonard Cohen*, "Interlude: Leonard Cohen the Cohen," 218–21. In
    "The Prophetic Mr. Cohen," Jackson states that Cohen sometimes signed his
    emails with a graphic of the priestly blessing.

42 Romans 15:33.

43 1 Corinthians 16:22b.

44 "You Want It Darker," *The Flame*, 143.

CHAPTER TEN

1   "Different Sides," *The Flame*, 120. See also Freedman, *Leonard Cohen*, 131–9, and Jackson, "The Prophetic Mr. Cohen."

2   Devlin, *Leonard Cohen: In His Own Words*, 11.

3   https://www.leonardcohenfiles.com/doron-amsterdam.pdf, 4.

4   1 Thessalonians 4:17 is just one example.

5   "The Future," *Stranger Music*, 372.

6   "My Guitar Stood Up Today," *The Flame*, 68.

7   Stendahl, *Paul among Jews and Gentiles*.

8   *The Flame*, 267. I have not had opportunity in this book to discuss the extremely important influence Lorca had on Cohen (who named his daughter after the Spanish poet and playwright). That influence shows up in everything from Leonard's masculinity to his ascetic impulses. For more on Lorca's influence, see Simmons, *I'm Your Man*, 28–30, and Freedman, *Leonard Cohen*, 13–15.

9   See Richard Ascough's helpful comparison of individualist and collectivist ways of framing identity in *Lydia, Paul's Cosmopolitan Hostess*, 8–13.

10 *The Flame*, 115.

11 Heschmeyer, "Leonard Cohen, the Christ-Haunted."

12 Philippians 3:4b–5a.

13 See Moreton-Robinson, "Relationality," 69–77. It is interesting that some of Leonard's earliest memories are of visiting Kahnawà:ke Kanien'ke:ha (Mohawk) territory near Montreal, and that the Indigenous Saint Kateri had such influence on his thought. For more on this see Freedman, *Leonard Cohen*, 128–30.

14 Romans 8:23 (Paul uses adoption metaphors in Romans 8:15, 9:4 and Galatians 4:5). Lewis points out the allusions this metaphor would have had for Paul's hearers in *Paul's 'Spirit of Adoption' in Its Roman Imperial Context*.

15 McDonald, "Ex-Pagan Pagans?" 8.

16 1 Corinthians 15:10.

17 Casaliggi, *Legacies of Romanticism*.

18 "Did I Ever Love You," *The Flame*, 132.

19 Simmons, *I'm Your Man*, 423, 482.

20 Philippians 3:5b–6. See also 2 Corinthians 5:10–11.

21 1 Corinthians 2:3.

22 1 Corinthians 4:11–12a.

23 Some commentators point to Romans 7:15–25 as an example of such a "dark night of the soul" for Paul. However, I side with those who believe that here

he is talking about how the Torah upholds proper conduct. See Stendahl, *Paul among Jews and Gentiles*, 93–4.

24 1 Corinthians 15:20. "Fallen asleep" is in the Greek, while the NRSV correctly understands this as "died." On the significance of Jesus's resurrection as the beginning of a general resurrection, see Fredriksen, *Paul: The Pagan's Apostle*, 145.

25 *The Flame*, 267.

26 Gilmore, "Remembering the Life and Legacy."

27 Posner, "That's How the Light Gets In," 516, approvingly reports that Max Layton, son of the late Canadian poet Irving Layton, calls Cohen "the greatest psalmist since King David." Freedman, *Leonard Cohen*, 192, points out that Cohen's *Book of Mercy* (1984) was self-consciously modelled on the psalms.

28 2 Corinthians 12:7b–9a.

29 Nicolet-Anderson, "Leonard Cohen's Use of the Bible," 224.

30 "Anthem," *Stranger Music*, 373.

31 Posner, "That's How the Light Gets In," 513. See also Freedman, *Leonard Cohen*, 147–8.

32 Cohen's symbol of the "unified heart" was perhaps important to him also in this way.

33 The reunification of genders is spoken of at least as far back as the Greek playwright Aristophanes.

34 2 Corinthians 4:7–9.

35 Mus and Trehearne, *The Demons of Leonard Cohen*, 154.

36 "Treaty," *The Flame*, 147.

37 "It Seemed the Better Way," *The Flame*, 154.

38 *The Flame*, 160.

39 Freedman, *Leonard Cohen*, 238.

40 "Treaty," *The Flame*, 146–7.

41 From a letter by Leonard Cohen to his son in Wieseltier, "My Friend Leonard Cohen."

42 *The Flame*, 277.

43 Simmons, *I'm Your Man*, 509.

CHAPTER ELEVEN

1 Burger and Hahn, *Leonard Cohen on Leonard Cohen*, 538 (emphasis added).

2 Wieseltier, "My Friend Leonard Cohen."

3 On the importance of reception and of reception communities for the legacy of artists, including in popular music, see Partridge, *The Lyre of Orpheus*, 57.

4   Cohen would likely have agreed that his ability to "ensure his public legacy" is still very much an indication of elite privilege attached to his gender, nationality, and birth.

5   Romans 5:3–5.

6   Freedman, *Leonard Cohen*, 234–5.

7   The phrase "meeting X again for the first time" comes from Borg, *Meeting Jesus Again for the First Time.*

8   Partridge, *The Lyre of Orpheus*, 48.

9   National Film Board of Canada, "Ladies and Gentlemen."

10 For a nuancing of ancient ideas of individual and community, see Maier, "Paul's Letter to Philemon," 524.

11 Stendahl, *Paul among Jews and Gentiles*, 125.

12 Simmons, *I'm Your Man*, 268.

13 "Leaving the Table," *The Flame*, 150.

14 Freedman, *Leonard Cohen*, 239; Jackson, "The Prophetic Mr. Cohen."

15 See Padgett's *I'm Your Fan.*

16 One of the most glaring and incontrovertible differences between the genuine letters of Paul and the pseudo-Pauline letters is their diametrically opposite view of gender and marriage. For a book-length treatment of these differences, see Beattie, *Women and Marriage in Paul.*

17 Romans 12:14–17.

18 1 Thessalonians 5:26–7.

19 https://unifiedheartproductionsfoundation.org/.

20 Partridge, *The Lyre of Orpheus*, 41–2.

21 "Crazy to Love You," *The Flame*, 115.

22 "You Got Me Singing," *The Flame*, 140.

23 Given Phil Spector's involvement, many (perhaps Leonard himself) would prefer that album not come up at all.

24 1 Corinthians 13:4–8a.

25 See 1 Corinthians 7:26–38: "he who marries his fiancé does well; and he who refrains from marriage will do better."

26 https://www.cbc.ca/arts/this-ghostly-projection-of-leonard-cohen-s-su- zanne-is-a-reminder-to-slow-down-and-breathe-1.5833168?cmp=FB_Post_ Arts. The "tea and oranges" inspiration was apparently Constant Comment herbal tea. See Devlin, *Leonard Cohen: In His Own Words*, 57.

27 See MacDonald, "Rereading Paul," 236–53.

28 Warren, "My OTP: Harry Potter Fanfiction and the Old Testament Pseude- pigrapha." Also de Bruin, "Nostalgia, Novelty, and the Subversion."

29 1 Timothy 2:15.

30 On receptions of Paul throughout history, see Harrill, *Paul the Apostle*, 138–62.

31 Freedman makes the same point in *Leonard Cohen*, 245–6.

32 Castelli, "Paul on Women and Gender," 223.

33 Freedman, *Leonard Cohen*, 238.

34 "Beside the Shepherd," *Let Us Compare Mythologies*, 59.

35 1 Corinthians 15:50–52a.

36 Romans 15:33.

37 "August 2, 1976," *The Flame*, 263.

Bibliography

Anderson, Matthew R. "Judeophobia and Pauline Studies." In *Judeophobia and the New Testament,* edited by Eric Vanden Eykel, Sarah Rollens, and Meredith J.C. Warren. Grand Rapids, MI: Eerdmans, 2023.

–. "Paul and Pauline Epistles." *The Encyclopedia of Ancient History*. Hoboken, NJ: Wiley-Blackwell, 2022.

Anderson, R. Dean, Jr. *Ancient Rhetorical Theory and Paul.* Rev. ed. Leuven, BE: Peeters, 1999.

Ascough, Richard S. *Lydia: Paul's Cosmopolitan Hostess.* Paul's Social Network: Brothers and Sisters in Faith. Collegeville, MN: Liturgical Press, 2009.

Avery-Peck, Alan J. "Seven Heavens." In *The Jewish Annotated New Testament. Second Edition. NRSV Version,* edited by Amy-Jill Levine and Marc Zvi Brettler, 370. Oxford: Oxford University Press, 2017.

Barclay, John M.G. "Mirror-Reading a Polemical Letter: Galatians as a Test Case." *Journal for the Study of the New Testament* 10, no. 31 (1987): 73–93.

Bassler, Jouette M. "First Corinthians." In *Women's Bible Commentary,* 3rd ed., edited by Carol A. Newsom, Sharon H. Ringe, and Jacqueline E. Lapsey, 557–65. Louisville, KY: Westminster/John Knox, 2012.

Beattie, Gillian. *Women and Marriage in Paul and His Early Interpreters.* London: T&T Clark International, 2005.

Berger, Theresa. "Women's Liturgical Practices and Leadership Roles in Early Christian Communities." In *Patterns of Women's Leadership in Early Christianity,* edited by Joan E. Taylor and Ilaria L.E. Ramelli, 180–94. Oxford: Oxford University Press, 2021.

Bhabha, Homi. "Of Mimicry and Man: The Ambivalence of Colonial Discourse." *October* 28 (Spring 1984): 125–33.

Bloom, Myra. "The Darker Side of Leonard Cohen: How the Myth of the Male Genius Shields Our Cultural Heroes from Scrutiny." *The Walrus,* 9 April 2018, updated 5 April 2021. https://thewalrus.ca/the-darker-side-of-leonard-cohen/.

Borg, Marcus. *Meeting Jesus Again for the First Time: The Historical Jesus and the Heart of Contemporary Faith.* San Francisco: Harper, 1994.

Boyarin, Daniel. "Body Politic among the Brides of Christ: Paul and the Origins of Christian Sexual Renunciation." In *Asceticism,* edited by Vincent L.

Wimbush and Richard Valantasis, 459–78. Oxford: Oxford University Press, 1995.

Brooten, Bernadette. "'Junia ... Outstanding among the Apostles' (Romans 16:7)." In *Women Priests: A Catholic Commentary on the Vatican Declaration,* edited by Leonard Swidler and Arlene Swidler, 141–4. Mahwah, NJ: Paulist, 1977.

Brown, Peter. *The Body and Society: Men, Women, and Sexual Renunciation in Early Christianity.* New York: Columbia University Press, 1988.

Burger, Jeff, and Jon Hahn. *Leonard Cohen on Leonard Cohen: Interviews and Encounters.* Chicago: Chicago Review Press, 2014.

Butler, Judith. *Undoing Gender.* New York: Routledge, 2004.

Caputo, John D. and Linda Martin Alcoff. *St. Paul among the Philosophers.* Indiana Series in the Philosophy of Religion. Bloomington: Indiana University Press, 2009.

Casaliggi, Carmen, and Paul March-Russell. *Legacies of Romanticism: Literature, Culture, Aesthetics.* Routledge Studies in Romanticism, 17. New York: Routledge, 2012.

Castelli, Elizabeth. "Disciplines of Difference: Asceticism and History in Paul." In *Asceticism and the New Testament,* edited by Leif E. Vaage and Vincent L. Wimbush, 171–85. New York: Routledge, 1999.

–. *Imitating Paul: A Discourse of Power.* Louisville, KY: Westminster/John Knox, 1991.

–. "'I Will Make Mary Male': Pieties of the Body and Gender Transformation of Christian Women in Late Antiquity." In *Body Guards: The Cultural Politics of Gender Ambiguity,* edited by Julia Epstein and Kristina Straub, 29–49. New York: Routledge, 1991.

–. "Paul on Women and Gender." In *Women and Christian Origins,* edited by Ross Shepard Kraemer and Mary Rose D'Angelo, 221–35. Oxford: Oxford University Press, 1999.

Cohen, Leonard. *Book of Longing.* London: Penguin, 2007.

–. *The Flame.* Edinburgh: Canongate Books, 2018.

–. *Let Us Compare Mythologies.* Edinburgh: Canongate Books, 2019. First published in 1956 by Contact Press.

–. *Stranger Music: Selected Poems and Songs.* London: Jonathan Cape Random House, 1993.

Concannon, Cavan W. "Paul and Authorship." *Bible Odyssey.* Society of Biblical Literature. https://www.bibleodyssey.org/people/related-articles/paul-and-authorship.

–. "'Not for an Olive Wreath, but Our Lives': Gladiators, Athletes, and Early Christian Bodies." *Journal of Biblical Literature* 133 no. 1 (2014): 193–214.

Conway, Colleen. *Behold the Man: Jesus and Greco-Roman Masculinity.* Oxford: Oxford University Press, 2008.

Curnyn, Sean. "Leonard Cohen, Religious Alchemist." *First Things,* 18 November 2016. https://www.firstthings.com/web-exclusives/2016/11/leonard-cohen-religious-alchemist.

D'Angelo, Mary R. "Roman 'Family Values' and the Apologetic Concerns of Philo and Paul: Reading the Sixth Commandment." *New Testament Studies* 61, no. 4 (2015): 525–46. https://doi.org/10.1017/S002868851500017X.

Davey, Wesley Thomas. "Playing Christ: Participation and Suffering in the Letters of Paul." *Currents in Biblical Research* 17, no. 3 (2019): 306–31.

De Bruin, Tom. "Nostalgia, Novelty, and the Subversion of Authority in Testaments of the Twelve Patriarchs." In *Fan Fiction and Ancient Scribal Cultures,* edited by Frauke Uhlenbruch, and Sonja Ammann. Special Issue of *Transformative Works and Cultures,* 31 (2019). https://doi.org/10.3983/twc.2019.1553.

Devlin, Jim. *Leonard Cohen: In His Own Words.* London: Omnibus, 1998.

Doering, Lutz. "The Commissioning of Paul: Light from the Prophet Jeremiah on the Self-Understanding of the Apostle?" In *Jeremiah's Scriptures,* edited by Hindy Najman and Konrad Schmid, 544–65. Leiden, BE: Brill, 2017.

–. "Early Judaism and Early Christianity." In *Early Judaism and Its Modern Interpreters,* Second Edition, edited by Matthias Henze and Rodney A. Werline, 541–65. Atlanta, GA: Society of Biblical Literature Press, 2020.

Donaldson, Terence L. *Gentile Christian Identity from Cornelius to Constantine: The Nations, the Parting of the Ways, and Roman Imperial Ideology.* Grand Rapids, MI: Eerdmans, 2020.

Dorman, Loranne S. and Clive L. Rawlins. *Leonard Cohen: Prophet of the Heart.* London: Omnibus, 1990.

Du Toit, Andrie P. "'In Christ,' 'in the Spirit,' and Related Prepositional Phrases: Their Relevance for a Discussion on Pauline Mysticism." *Neotestamentica* 34, no. 2 (2000): 287–98.

Eastman, David L. "The Pastoral Epistles." *Bible Odyssey.* Society of Biblical Literature. https://www.bibleodyssey.org/en/tools/video-gallery/p/pastoral-epistles.

Ehrensperger, Kathy. "Paul, the Man: Enigmatic Images." In *Gender and Second-Temple Judaism,* edited by Kathy Ehrensperger and Shayna Sheinfeld, 65–84. Lanham, MD: Lexington Books/Fortress Academic, 2020.

Ehrman, Bart D. *The New Testament: A Historical Introduction to the Early Christian Writings.* Seventh Edition. Oxford: Oxford University Press, 2020.

Eisenbaum, Pamela. *Paul Was Not a Christian: The Original Message of a Misunderstood Apostle.* San Francisco: HarperOne, 2009.

Emmett, Grace. "The Apostle Paul's Maternal Masculinity." *Journal of Early Christian History* 11, no. 1 (2021): 15–37.

Engberg-Pedersen, Troels. *Paul and the Stoics.* Edinburgh: T&T Clark, 2000.

Engels, Stacey. "From the Dark Green Hill to Our Lady of the Harbour." *International Journal of Religious Tourism and Pilgrimage* 7, no. 1 (2019): 116–22. https://arrow.tudublin.ie/ijrtp/vol7/iss1/12.

Erens, Pamela. "Old Ideas: Leonard Cohen's Legacy." *The Virginia Quarterly Review* 94, no. 3 (2018): 196–205.

Fredriksen, Paula. "If It Looks Like a Duck, and It Quacks Like a Duck: On *Not* Giving Up the Godfearers." In *A Most Reliable Witness: Essays in Honor of Ross Shepard Kraemer,* edited by S.A. Harvey, N.P. DesRosiers, S.L. Lander, J.Z. Pastis, and D. Ullucci, 25–33. Providence, RI: Brown University, 2015.

–. "Paul and Judaism." *Bible Odyssey.* Society of Biblical Literature. https://www.bibleodyssey.org/people/related-articles/paul-and-judaism.aspx.

–. *Paul: The Pagan's Apostle.* New Haven, CT: Yale University Press, 2017.

Freedman, Harry. *Leonard Cohen: The Mystical Roots of Genius.* London: Bloomsbury, 2021.

Frye, Northrop. *The Great Code: The Bible and Literature.* San Francisco: HarperOne, 2002.

Gager, John G. *Reinventing Paul.* Oxford: Oxford University Press, 2000.

Garroway, Joshua D. "Paul: Within Judaism, Without Law." In *Law and Lawlessness in Early Judaism and Early Christianity,* edited by David Lincicum, Ruth Sheridan, and Charles M. Stang, 49–66. Wissenschaftliche Untersuchungen Zum Neuen Testament, 420. Tübingen, DE: Mohr Siebeck, 2019.

Gauvreau, Michael. *The Catholic Origins of Quebec's Quiet Revolution, 1931–1970.* Montreal and Kingston: McGill-Queen's University Press, 2005.

Gilmore, Mikal. "Leonard Cohen: Remembering the Life and Legacy of the Poet of Brokenness." *Rolling Stone,* 30 November 2016. https://www.rollingstone.com/music/music-features/leonard-cohen-remembering-the-life-and-legacy-of-the-poet-of-brokenness-192994/.

Girard, Philippe. *Leonard Cohen: On a Wire.* Montreal: Drawn & Quarterly, 2021.

Glancy, Jennifer. "Slavery and the Rise of Christianity." In *The Cambridge World History of Slavery,* edited by K. Bradley and P. Cartledge, 456–81. Cambridge: Cambridge University Press, 2011.

Goff, Matthew. "The Mystery of God's Wisdom, the Parousia of a Messiah, and Visions of Heavenly Paradise." In *The Jewish Apocalyptic Tradition and the*

Shaping of New Testament Thought, edited by Benjamin E. Reynolds and Loren
    T. Stuckenbruck, 175–92. Minneapolis, MN: Augsburg-Fortress, 2017.

Grayston, Donald. "Monastic in His Own Way: Thomas Merton and Leonard
    Cohen," *The Merton Seasonal* 34, no. 3 (2009): 3–9. http://www.merton.org/
    ITMS/Seasonal/2009PresidentialAddress.pdf.

Harrill, J. Albert. *Paul the Apostle: His Life and Legacy in their Roman Context.*
    Cambridge: Cambridge University Press, 2012.

Harris, William V. *Ancient Literacy.* Cambridge, MA: Harvard University Press,
    1991.

Henze, Matthias. "Apocalyptic Literature." In *Early Judaism and Its Modern
    Interpreters,* Second Edition, edited by Matthias Henze and Rodney A.
    Werline, 405–35. Atlanta, GA: Society of Biblical Literature Press, 2020.

Heschmeyer, Joe. "Leonard Cohen, the Christ-Haunted." *First Things,* 17
    November 2016. https://www.firstthings.com/blogs/firstthoughts/2016/11/
    leonard-cohen-the-christ-haunted.

Horrell, David G. *An Introduction to the Study of Paul. Third Edition.* T&T Clark
    Approaches to Biblical Studies. London: Bloomsbury, 2015.

Jackson, Timothy P. "The Prophetic Mr. Cohen." In *Leonard Cohen and
    Philosophy: Various Positions,* edited by Jason Holt. Chicago: Open Court,
    2014.

Klein, A.M. *Literary Essays and Reviews.* Edited by Usher Caplan and M.W
    Steinberg. Collected Works of A.M. Klein. Toronto: Toronto University
    Press, 1987.

Larson, Jennifer. "Paul's Masculinity." *Journal of Biblical Literature* 23, no. 1 (2004):
    85–97.

Lebold, Christophe. "From Existential Troubadour to Crooner of Light: Uses
    and Refractions of the Love Song in Leonard Cohen's Work." *Rock Music
    Studies: Rock and Love* 5, no. 1 (2018): 1–19.

Lévi-Strauss, Claude. *Le Totémisme Aujourd'hui.* Paris: Presses Universitaires de
    France, 1962.

Lewis, Robert Brian. *Paul's 'Spirit of Adoption' in its Roman Imperial Context.*
    Library of New Testament Studies. London: Bloomsbury T&T Clark, 2016.

Lieber, Andrea. "Early Judaism and Mysticism." In *Early Judaism and Its Modern
    Interpreters,* 2nd ed., edited by Matthias Henze and Rodney A. Werline,
    519–40. Atlanta, GA: Society of Biblical Literature Press, 2020.

Longenecker, Bruce. "Salvation History in Galatians and the Making of a
    Pauline Discourse." *Journal for the Study of Paul and His Letters* 2, no. 2 (2012):
    65–87.

Lopez, Davina. "Paul." *Bible Odyssey*. Society of Biblical Literature. https://www.bibleodyssey.org/people/main-articles/paul.

Luther, Martin, Brooks Schramm, and Kirsi Irmeli Stjerna. *Martin Luther, the Bible, and the Jewish People: A Reader*. Minneapolis, MN: Fortress Press, 2012.

MacDonald, Margaret Y. "Rereading Paul: Early Interpreters of Paul on Women and Gender." In *Women and Christian Origins*, edited by Ross Shepard Kraemer and Mary Rose D'Angelo, 236–53. Oxford: Oxford University Press, 1999.

Maier, Harry O. "Paul's Letter to Philemon: A Case Study in Individualisation, Dividuation, and Partibility in Imperial Spatial Contexts." In *Religious Individualisation*, edited by Martin Fuchs et. al., 519–40. Berlin: Walter de Gruyter, 2019.

Marchal, Joseph A. *Appalling Bodies*. Oxford: Oxford University Press, 2020.

–. "Queer Studies and Critical Masculinity Studies." In *Feminist Biblical Studies in the 20th Century: Scholarship and Movement*, edited by Elisabeth Schüssler Fiorenza, 261–80. Atlanta, GA: Society of Biblical Literature, 2014.

May, Elaine Tyler. *Homeward Bound: American Families in the Cold War Era*. New York: Basic Books, 1988.

McDonald, Denys N. "'Ex-Pagan Pagans'? Paul, Philo, and Gentile Ethnic Reconfiguration." *Journal for the Study of the New Testament* (March 2022): 1–28.

Mersereau, Bob. "Great Moments in Canadian Music (Track 3): Cohen's Comeback – How a Tribute Album Revived Leonard Cohen's Career." *National Music Centre Amplify*, 7 November 2019. https://amplify.nmc.ca/great-moments-in-canadian-music-track-3-cohens-comeback-how-a-tribute-album-revived-leonard-cohens-career/.

Morray-Jones, C.R.A. "Paradise Revisited (2 Cor 12:1–12): The Jewish Mystical Background of Paul's Apostolate." *Harvard Theological Review* 86, no. 3 (1993): 265–92.

Moreton-Robinson, Aileen. "Relationality." In *Sources and Methods in Indigenous Studies*, edited by Chris Andersen and Jean M. O'Brien, 69–77. London: Routledge, 2016.

Mus, Francis, and Brian Trehearne. *The Demons of Leonard Cohen*. Translated by Laura Vroomen. Études Canadiennes. Ottawa: Presses de l'Université d'Ottawa/ University of Ottawa Press, 2020.

Nanos, Mark D. "Reading the Antioch Incident (Gal 2:11-21) as a Subversive Banquet Narrative." *Journal for the Study of Paul and His Letters* 7, no. 1–2 (2017): 26–52.

National Film Board of Canada. "Ladies and Gentlemen ... Mr Leonard Cohen," Directed by Donald Brittain and Don Owen, NFB, 1965. Documentary.

Neutel, Karin B. *A Cosmopolitan Ideal: Paul's Declaration 'Neither Jew nor Greek, Neither Slave nor Free, nor Male and Female' in the Context of First-Century Thought.* London: Bloomsbury T&T Clark, 2016.

Nicolet-Anderson, Valérie. "Leonard Cohen's Use of the Bible: Transformations of the Sacred." *Biblical Reception* 3 (2014): 223–39.

–. "Cohen, Leonard." In *The Oxford Encyclopedia of the Bible and the Arts.* Oxford University Press, 2015. https://www-oxfordreference-com.lib-ezproxy. concordia.ca/view/10.1093/acref:obso/9780199846511.001.0001/acref-9780199846511-e-33.

Norton, Jonathan D.H., Garrick Allen, Lindsey A. Askin, eds. *Reading, Writing and Bookish Circles in the Ancient Mediterranean.* New York: Bloomsbury, 2022.

Novenson, Matthew. "Did Paul Abandon Either Judaism or Monotheism?" In *The New Cambridge Companion to St. Paul,* edited by B.W. Longenecker, 239–59. Cambridge: Cambridge University Press.

O'Brian, Robert. "Songs and Thoughts of Leonard Cohen." Interview, January 1987. http://robertobrianinterviews.blogspot.com/2011/12/leonard-cohen. html.

Olbricht, Thomas H. and Jerry L. Sumney. *Paul and Pathos.* Atlanta, GA: Society of Biblical Literature, 2001.

O'Neil, Mary Anne. "Leonard Cohen, Singer of the Bible." *Cross Currents* 65, no. 1 (March 2015): 91–9.

Padgett, Ray. *I'm Your Fan: The Songs of Leonard Cohen.* London: Bloomsbury Academic, 2020.

Parks, Sara. "Because of Her We All Die: Eve in Early Jewish and Early Christian Reception." In *The Routledge Companion to Eve,* edited by Caroline Blyth and Emily Colgan. London: Routledge, 2023.

–. *Gender in the Rhetoric of Jesus: Women in Q.* Lanham, KY: Lexington, 2019.

–. "Women and Gender in the Apocrypha." In *The Oxford Handbook of the Apocrypha,* edited by Gerbern Oegema, 477–97. Oxford: Oxford University Press, 2021.

Parks, Sara, Shayna Sheinfeld, and Meredith J.C. Warren. *Jewish and Christian Women in the Ancient Mediterranean.* London: Routledge, 2022.

Partridge, Christopher H. *The Lyre of Orpheus: Popular Music, the Sacred, and the Profane.* New York: Oxford University Press, 2014.

Pleshoyano, Alexandra. « La poésie lyrique de Leonard Cohen : lieu d'un déploiement de la mystique juive ». *Théologiques* 18, no. 2 (2010): 163–86.

–. "Leonard Cohen's *Poiesis*: Toward the Unified Heart Where All Bounds Fade Away." In *Mystic Musings in Art and Poetry,* edited by Kurian Kachappilly, 13–38. New Delhi: Christian World Imprints, 2013.

Porter, Stanley E. "Ancient Literate Culture and Popular Rhetorical Knowledge: Implications for Studying Pauline Rhetoric," in *Paul and Ancient Rhetoric: Theory and Practice in the Hellenistic Context*, edited by Stanley E. Porter and Bryan R. Dyer, 96–116. Cambridge: Cambridge University Press, 2016.

Posner, Michael. *Leonard Cohen, Untold Stories*. 3 vols. New York: Simon & Schuster, 2020–22.

–. "That's How the Light Gets In: Remembering Leonard Cohen." *Queen's Quarterly* (Winter 2017): 510–25.

Probst, Christopher J. *Demonizing the Jews: Luther and the Protestant Church in Nazi Germany*. Bloomington: Indiana University Press, 2012.

Reinhartz, Adele. "A Fork in the Road or a Multi-Lane Highway? New Perspectives on the 'Parting of the Ways' between Judaism and Christianity." In *The Changing Face of Judaism, Christianity, and Other Greco-Roman Religions in Antiquity*, edited by Ian H. Henderson, Gerbern Oegema, and Sara Parks Ricker, 280–95. Gütersloh, DE: Gütersloher Verlagshaus, 2006.

Roetzel, Calvin J. "Sex and the Single God: Celibacy as Social Deviancy in the Roman Period." In *Text and Artifact in the Religions of Mediterranean Antiquity: Essays in Honour of Peter Richardson*, edited by Stephen G. Wilson and Michel R. Desjardins, 231–48. Waterloo, ON: Wilfrid Laurier University Press, 2000.

Rohter, Larry. "On the Road, for Reasons Both Practical and Spiritual." *New York Times*, 25 February 2009, 2. https://www.nytimes.com/2009/02/25/arts/music/25cohe.html.

Rosen-Zvi, Ishay. "Early Judaism and Rabbinic Judaism." In *Early Judaism and Its Modern Interpreters*, Second Edition, edited by Matthias Henze and Rodney A. Werline, 489–518. Atlanta, GA: Society of Biblical Literature Press, 2020.

Schellenberg, Ryan S. *Rethinking Paul's Rhetorical Education*. Atlanta, GA: Society of Biblical Literature Press, 2013.

Schneller, Johanna. "Cohen's Tales of Seduction Look Different through a #MeToo Lens." *Globe & Mail*, 8 December 2020. https://www.theglobeandmail.com/arts/article-leonard-cohens-tales-of-seduction-look-different-through-a-metoo/.

Schweitzer, Albert. *The Mysticism of Paul the Apostle*. Translated by Wm. Montgomery. London: A&C Black, 1931.

Seesengood, Robert Paul. "'Not Grudgingly, nor under Compulsion': Love, Labor, Service, and Slavery in Pauline Rhetoric." In *Reading with Feeling: Affect Theory and the Bible*, edited by Fiona C. Black and Jennifer L. Koosed,

141–56. Semeia Studies 95. Atlanta, GA: Society of Biblical Literature Press, 2019.

Segal, Alan F. "Mysticism." In *The Eerdman's Dictionary of Early Judaism*, edited by John J. Collins and Daniel C. Harlow, 982–6. Grand Rapids, MI: Eerdmans, 2010.

Shapiro, Gary. "The End of the World and Other Times in *The Future*." In *Leonard Cohen and Philosophy: Various Positions*, edited by Jason Holt. Chicago: Open Court, 2014.

Simmons, Sylvie. *I'm Your Man: The Life of Leonard Cohen*. London: Vintage Press, 2012/2017.

Soon, Isaac. "The Short Apostle: The Stature of Paul in Light of 2 Cor 11:33 and the Acts of Paul and Thecla." *Early Christianity* 12, no. 2 (2021): 159–78.

Stendahl, Krister. *Paul among Jews and Gentiles*. Minneapolis, MN: Fortress Press, 1976.

Stewart, Eric C. "Masculinity in the New Testament and Early Christianity." *Biblical Theology Bulletin* 46, no. 2 (2016): 91–102.

Sulzbach, Carla. "When Going on a Heavenly Journey, Travel Light and Dress Appropriately." *Journal for the Study of the Pseudepigrapha* 19, no. 3 (2010): 163–93.

Taylor, Joan E. "Male-Female Missionary Pairings among Jesus' Disciples." In *Patterns of Women's Leadership in Early Christianity,* edited by Joan E. Taylor and Ilaria L.E. Ramelli, 29–49. Oxford: Oxford University Press, 2021.

Thiessen, Matthew. *Contesting Conversion: Genealogy, Circumcision, and Identity in Ancient Judaism and Christianity*. New York: Oxford University Press, 2011.

–. *Paul and the Gentile Problem*. New York: Oxford University Press, 2016.

Tolmie, D.F. "How Onesimus Was Heard – Eventually. Some Insights from the History of Interpretation of Paul's Letter to Philemon." *Acta Theologica* Sup27 (2019): 101–17.

Vaage, Leif E., and Vincent L. Wimbush, eds. *Asceticism and the New Testament*. New York: Routledge, 1999.

Warren, Meredith. "My OTP: Harry Potter Fanfiction and the Old Testament Pseudepigrapha." *Scriptura: Nouvelle Serie* 8, no. 1 (2006): 53–66.

Wieseltier, Leon. "My Friend Leonard Cohen: Darkness and Praise." *New York Times*, 14 November 2016. https://www.nytimes.com/2016/11/14/opinion/my-friend-leonard-cohen-darkness-and-praise.html?partner=rss&emc=rss.

Index

Subject Index

A36cts, 14, 84, 135n14
aging, 4, 8, 10, 42, 44, 70, 123
aloofness, 41, 43–4, 68
ambiguity
    poetic, 79, 83–4, 107, 129
    between spiritual and artistic
        and erotic drives, 44, 65, 92
anaphora, 77
Anderson, Matthew R., 3–9, 121
anti-Semitism, 17, 25, 84, 127, 129
Aristotle, 64
artifice
    Leonard, 18, 43, 113, 119, 121–2
    persona, 4, 5, 7, 10, 44
    See also rhetoric
asceticism, 55–62
    discipline, 55–9, 71
    higher love, 45
    in marriage, 11, 51–2, 71
    sexuality, 11, 41, 52, 55, 57–8
    societal aspects, 61
    See also celibacy
authenticity
    individual, 109
    of Pauline letters, 48–9

Ben Sirach, 69
biography, 10, 14, 32
blessedness, 26, 69, 116, 142n35
blessing
    by *cohenim*, 91, 104, 153n41
    in conclusion, 104, 131

    of enemies, 83, 124
    via sacrifice, 91
brokenness, 111–18
    and the cross, 30–2, 35, 37
    giving voice to, 9, 13, 23, 113–14, 118
    healing/repair of, 92, 114–15, 117, 142n25
    in Jewish tradition, 104, 114–16,
        153n39
    and pathos, 112
    praise in the face of, 118
    See also suffering
Buddhism
    as complementary to Judaism, 18,
        22–3, 57, 139n22
    as epochal Western trend, 58
    practice of, 18, 22, 56–7, 109

celibacy
    and aloofness, 41, 68
    and gendered self-control, 43
    not the whole of asceticism, 58
    pastoral epistles' attitude towards, 49
    societal aspects of, 58
    spiritual valuation of, 11, 50, 58, 128
    See also asceticism
Christ-assemblies
    non-Jews in, 19–20
    term explained, 137n40
    See also by name
Christianity
    anachronistically associated with
        Paul, 19, 23, 107

Index of Ancient Writings

Index of Leonard Cohen's Poetry